7-String GUITAR

by Andy Martin

ISBN 978-0-634-01576-2

HAL•LEONARD®
CORPORATION
7777 W. BLUEMOUND RD. P.O. BOX 13819 MILWAUKEE, WI 53213

Visit Hal Leonard Online at
www.halleonard.com

This book is dedicated in loving memory
to an amazing pianist and mother
My angel from up above
Grace Marie Martin

Seven-String Guitar

Table of Contents

Acknowledgments

Judy Martin, Family, friends, and all my students who gave me the opportunity to educate their minds and ears. Alex "weegee board" Salzman, Michael Huey and Rockin' House Entertainment, Tim Phouts and S.I.T. strings, Steve Blucher and DiMarzio, Dennis Levy and Levy's Leathers, Gerry Griffin, Scott Gilfix and Eventide, Cakewalk, all at Hal Leonard Corp., Rob Nishida and Ibanez Guitars, Neil Zlozower, and Steve Vai.

About the Author

Andy Martin began playing the guitar in his early teens. He was exposed to music at an early age by his mother, who often played classical piano for him. His teenage years were dedicated to practicing his instrument for up to 16 hours a day while studying theory, ear training, composition, and improvisation with Linc Chamberland, Ted Greene, and Chris Risola. Andy eventually developed a unique technique that he calls "Tabletop Guitar," which allows him to play the melody, chords, and bass all at the same time. He adapted this style from watching his mother use both hands on the piano.

Andy's compositions come from within, as he considers harmonic content a part of his soul and a building block for what he calls "melodic instrumental mood music featuring two-handed tapping technique with an emphasis on rock." In his compositions, one can hear influences from such greats as Steve Vai, Joe Satriani, Yngwie Malmsteen, Eric Johnson, Larry Carlton, Brahms, and Vivaldi.

After spending the last few years touring, Andy currently resides in Los Angeles, where he continues to compose, record, and teach. He is very particular about his equipment and proudly endorses Ibanez Guitars, Eventide Processors, S.I.T. strings, DiMarzio, Cakewalk, and Levy's Leathers.

To contact Andy Martin for more information or to comment on this publication you can e-mail him at *Andy@andymartinmusic.com*. Or visit his website at *www.andymartinmusic.com*.

Photo by Neil Zlozower

Introduction

The seven-string guitar has been around for a while, and its popularity has been increasing over the last few years. Many popular guitarists such as Munky and Head from Korn, Wes Borland from Limp Bizkit, John Petrucci from Dream Theater, George Van Eps, Jerry Sims, Andy Timmons, and, of course, Steve Vai use seven-string guitars as a primary instrument. As you may be able to guess from the variety of styles represented in this list, learning how to play the seven-string guitar can expand any player's repertoire. It is my hope that *Seven String Guitar* will help you do the same.

Seven String Guitar is primarily a reference book—a fountain of knowledge. In this book, you will learn chords, arpeggios, pentatonic scales, and the modes as they are adapted for the seven-string. There are many charts and fingerings throughout this book, and although learning different chord inversions and fingerings is essential for becoming a great guitarist, they are fairly worthless by themselves. Each chord, arpeggio, and scale in this book has a specific usage, or habitude, in our language. With patience, self-discipline, and practice, you will learn how to apply the proper usage in any musical situation. It is much better to know a few chords or fingerings, and use them in proper harmonic content than to know multiple chords and fingerings, and not use them in proper harmonic content. So as you use this book, be sure to spend enough time exploring each new item you learn in order to completely absorb it and understand it.

At first, you may feel intimidated or apprehensive about learning the seven-string guitar. After all, most people feel it's hard enough to play a six-string. But I believe that after spending only a short time with the instrument, you'll notice that it feels very natural and comfortable. Rather than feeling like a conventional six-string with an added string, it should be its own instrument. And with time, I'm sure it will.

Enjoy!

How to Approach this Book

Though this book is primarily a reference for seven-string guitar, with a little work, you can take it to the next level. Throughout this book, you should always focus on *listening* to the chord, arpeggio, or scale that you are playing. Train your ears to get familiar with these sounds. This is called *solfedge*. Your ears are your most important tool when learning a new language. Like colors in a visual spectrum, music has colors in the audible spectrum. Red, orange, yellow, green, blue, and violet are the spectrum of visuals, and notes (e.g., A, B, C, D, E, F, and G) make up the spectrum of audibles. Just as your eyes have been trained to recognize visual colors, your ears should be trained to recognize audible colors. If you do this, the day will come when you will be listening to music at home, or in your car, and you'll be able to identify the chord, progression, and key signature just from listening to it.

Recognize the tools you've been blessed with to play music. We all have two hands, 10 fingers, two ears, and, most importantly, a heart. Use them all to their fullest, and train them to their extremes. I believe that, as musicians, we can play or learn anything in our language. But also realize that each individual's interpretation will be slightly different because it's very hard to copy someone's heart and soul.

To get the most out of this book, it is highly recommended that you:

- Be willing to practice religiously. Make a routine and stick to it. Whatever time you have available should be dedicated to learning our language. Be willing to expand your knowledge because, at any level, you can (and will) always learn more whether you're studying theory, technique, or improvisation. Your practicing should cover all areas, including rhythm, chords, solfedge, scales, picking techniques, two-handed tapping, improvisation, and phrasing. In short, practice everything.

- Approach this book in its proper order: front-to-back. You can use it as a reference, but if you don't know some of the language, you might miss out on some important terminology.

- Know your basic music theory on chords and arpeggios, and how they are derived from modes. You should also know how to read music. Many players *think* they know how to read music, but unless you are able to pick up a piece of sheet music and read it like a book (i.e., you can actually hear the music in your minds ear as you read), you need to work on your reading skills.

- Listen to all styles of music so you can understand what the material in this book sounds like, and can use the material in its proper context. An effective way to learn our language is by what I first addressed at the top of the page, which is listening to a chord, arpeggio, or scale until you can identify it. After repeatedly listening to a chord, it will gradually seep into your mind's ear, and through "mental osmosis," become part of you.

- Have patience, dedication, and discipline.

Remember, patience is a major part of learning a new language. Before you can break the rules, you have to know them. A teacher of mine once said to me: "Learn to master your instrument, then master the music. Then, forget about everything, and just play your instrument."

Getting Started

The main attraction of the seven-string guitar is its expanded sonic range. The addition of a low B string has benefits for any style of music. In heavy metal, for example, it adds a much-desired boost to the bottom end of the guitar signal, beefing up even the heaviest of riffs and making power chords rumble in the mix. If you're a jazzer, the seven-string expands your capacity for walking bass lines, voice leading, pedal tones, and contrary motion within the harmony.

Below you'll see a fingerboard chart for the seven-string guitar. On it, all the notes are labeled for easy reference. If you don't already know the notes on your guitar's neck, begin memorizing them now. It will make your learning experience much richer and more satisfying. On the other hand, if you already know the notes on a standard six-string fretboard, your work is already done because there's a B string on it already (2nd string), only two octaves higher!

Seven String Fretboard

String Number →	7	6	5	4	3	2	1
Open Strings →	B	E	A	D	G	B	E
1	C	F	A#/Bb	D#/Eb	G#/Ab	C	F
2	C#/Db	F#/Gb	B	E	A	C#/Db	F#/Gb
3	D	G	C	F	A#/Bb	D	G
4	D#/Eb	G#/Ab	C#/Db	F#/Gb	B	D#/Eb	G#/Ab
5	E	A	D	G	C	E	A
6	F	A#/Bb	D#/Eb	G#/Ab	C#/Db	F	A#/Bb
7	F#/Gb	B	E	A	D	F#/Gb	B
8	G	C	F	A#/Bb	D#/Eb	G	C
9	G#/Ab	C#/Db	F#/Gb	B	E	G#/Ab	C#/Db
10	A	D	G	C	F	A	D
11	A#/Bb	D#/Eb	G#/Ab	C#/Db	F#/Gb	A#/Bb	D#/Eb
12	B	E	A	D	G	B	E

etc.

Chords

Chords are simply a group of scale tones played simultaneously. In this chapter, you will learn many types of chords such as: major, minor, major 7th, minor 7th, dominant 7th, and a legion more. Remember, memorization plays a significant role for these chord forms—not just for your mind, but more importantly for your ears. You'll want to train your ears to recognize these sounds—solfedge. A good, solid knowledge of chords will not only help your chordal/rhythm playing, it will also strengthen your lead playing.

Below is a table containing the chord types, intervallic formulas, chord symbols, and chord names that will be covered throughout this book (examples in key of C). It is important to meticulously review and comprehend these symbols before proceeding through this chapter.

CHORD TYPE	FORMULA	NOTES	CHORD NAME
Fifth	1–5	C–G	C5
Major	1–3–5	C–E–G	C
Major, added ninth	1–3–5–9	C–E–G–D	Cadd9
Suspended fourth	1–4–5	C–F–G	Csus4
Suspended second	1–2–5	C–D–G	Csus2
Sixth	1–3–5–6	C–E–G–A	C6
Major seventh	1–3–5–7	C–E–G–B	Cmaj7
Major seventh, sharp eleventh	1–3–5–7–♯11	C–E–G–B–F♯	Cmaj7♯11
Major thirteenth	1–3–5–7–9–13	C–E–G–B–D–A	Cmaj13
Major ninth	1–3–5–7–9	C–E–G–B–D	Cmaj9
Minor, added ninth	1–♭3–5–9	C–E♭–G–D	Cm(add9)
Minor	1–♭3–5	C–E♭–G	Cm
Minor sixth	1–♭3–5–6	C–E♭–G–A	Cm6
Minor ninth	1–♭3–5–♭7–9	C–E♭–G–B♭–D	Cm9
Diminished	1–♭3–♭5	C–E♭–G♭	C°
Minor seventh, flat fifth	1–♭3–♭5–♭7	C–E♭–G♭–B♭	Cm7♭5
Minor seventh	1–♭3–5–♭7	C–E♭–G–B♭	Cm7
Minor ninth, major seventh	1–♭3–5–7–9	C–E♭–G–B–D	Cm9(maj7)
Minor eleventh	1–♭3–5–♭7–9–11	C–E♭–G–B♭–D–F	Cm11
Minor, major seventh	1–♭3–5–7	C–E♭–G–B	Cm(maj7)
Seventh, suspended fourth	1–4–5–♭7	C–F–G–B♭	C7sus4
Seventh, sharp ninth	1–3–5–♭7–♯9	C–E–G–B♭–D♯	C7♯9
Dominant seventh	1–3–5–♭7	C–E–G–B♭	C7
Augmented	1–3–♯5	C–E–G♯	C+
Ninth	1–3–5–♭7–9	C–E–G–B♭–D	C9

Power Chords

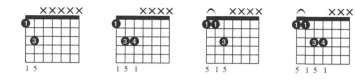

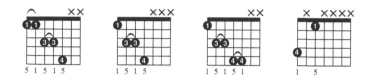

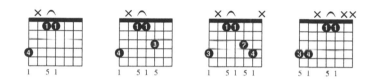

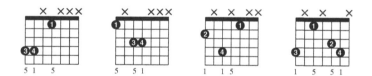

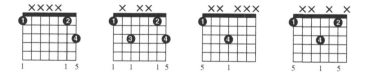

Notice that the theory and harmony of chord construction is the same for the seven-string as it is the six-string (or the piano, for that matter). So the only real difference between chords on a seven-string and chords on a six-string is the physical layout of the notes on the fretboard.

All of the chords in this book will be accompanied by an easy-to-read chord grid. The seven vertical lines of the grid represent the seven strings of the guitar, from low B to high E, moving left to right. The horizontal lines represent the frets. Chords containing notes above the fifth fret use a fret number (e.g., "7 fr") to the right of the chord grid to indicate where the chord is played.

xs tell you a string should not be played or should be muted.

os indicate an open string.

A dark, thick line represents the **nut** on the guitar. →

A **barre** (pronounced like "bar") is shown when a finger holds down two or more strings at the same time.

Black **dots** indicate the notes to be played, as well → as their location on the fretboard. **Numbers** tell you what fingers to use to fret the strings. Think of your left-hand fingers as being numbered 1 through 4 and your thumb labeled as "T."

Note intervals appear below each string to help you understand the voicing.

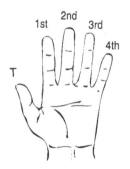

All of the chords in this book (with the exception of the Open Derivative chords) are moveable. That is, you can slide them up and down the fingerboard to other keys, and the new chord is simply called by its root note. So, if you learn a Cmaj7 chord with the root on the seventh string at the first fret, and slide the form up two frets, you now are playing a Dmaj7 chord.

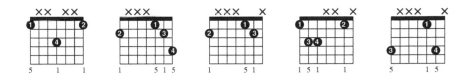

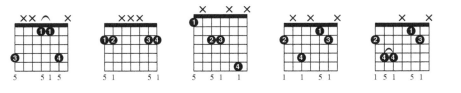

Open Derivative

Key of A

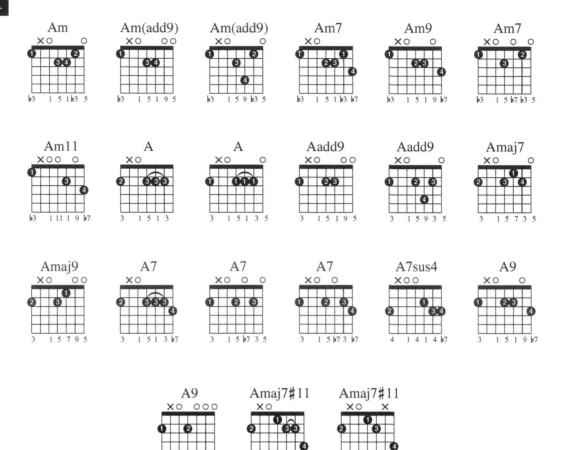

Key of B

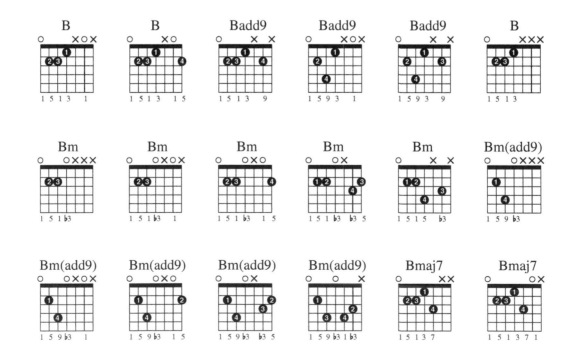

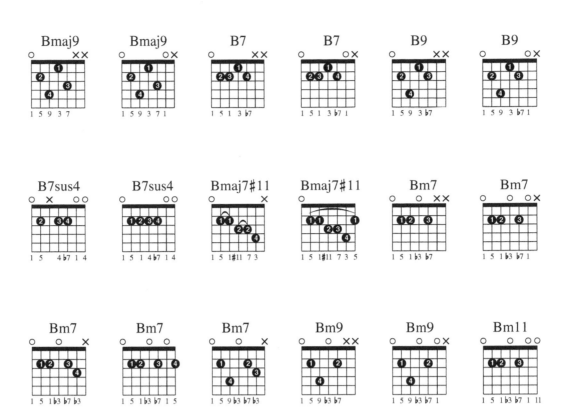

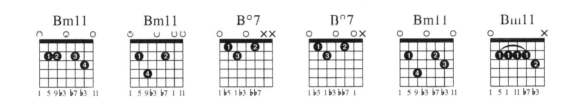

Key of C

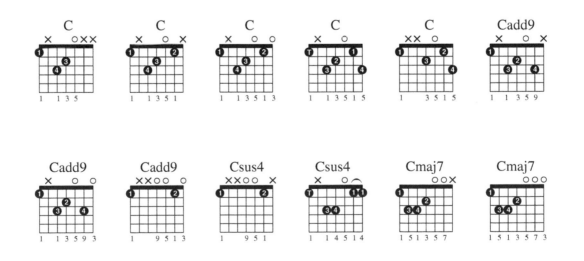

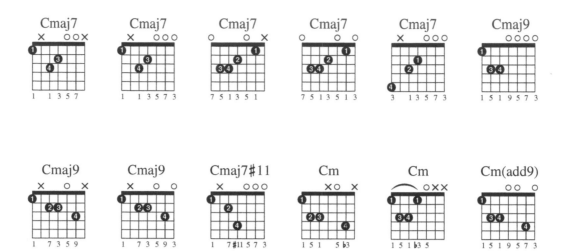

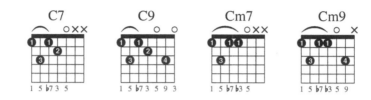

Key of D

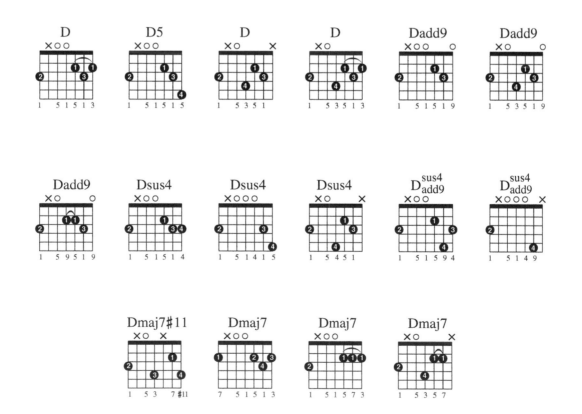

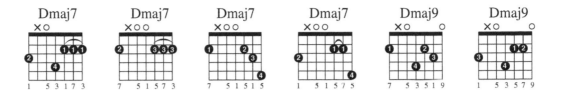

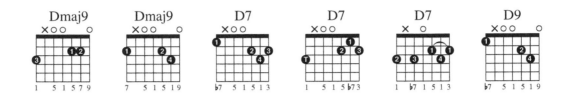

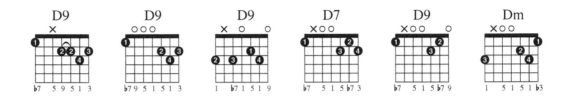

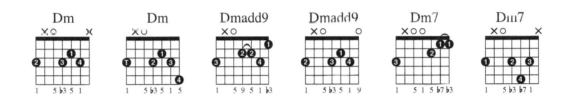

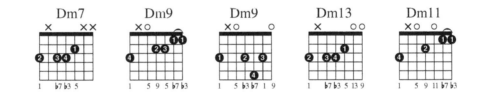

Key of E

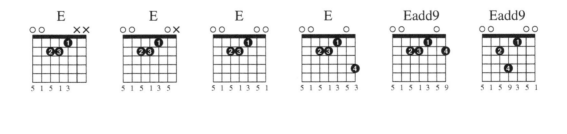

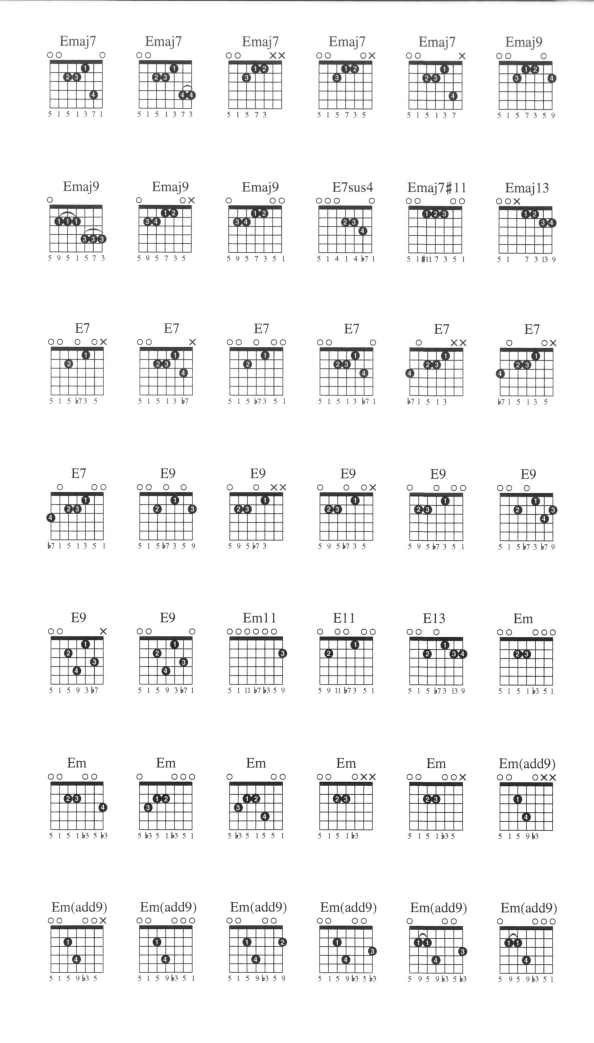

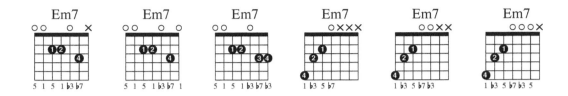

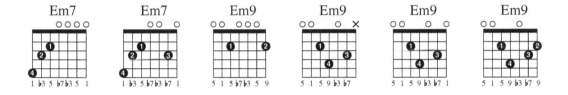

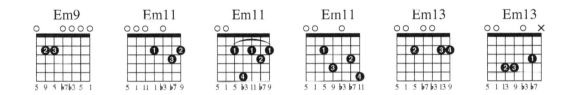

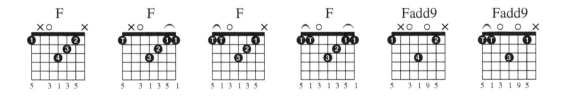

Key of F

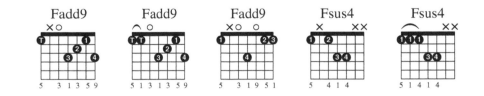

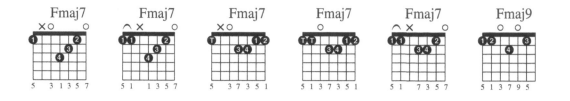

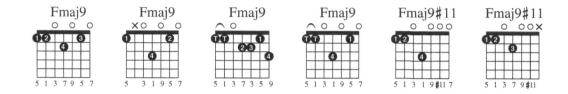

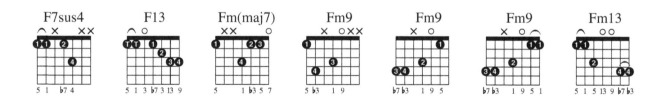

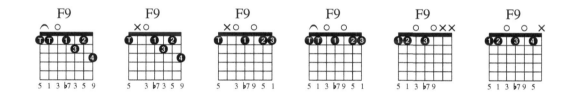

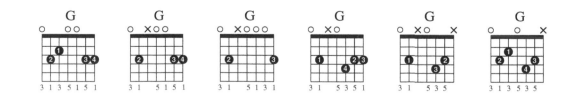

Key of G

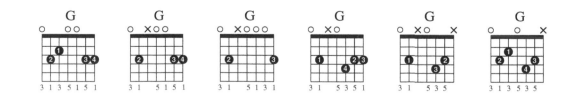

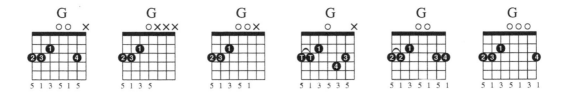

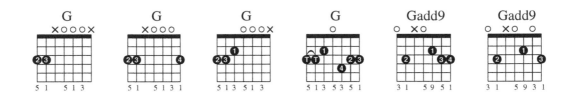

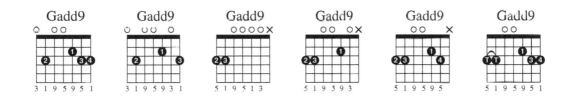

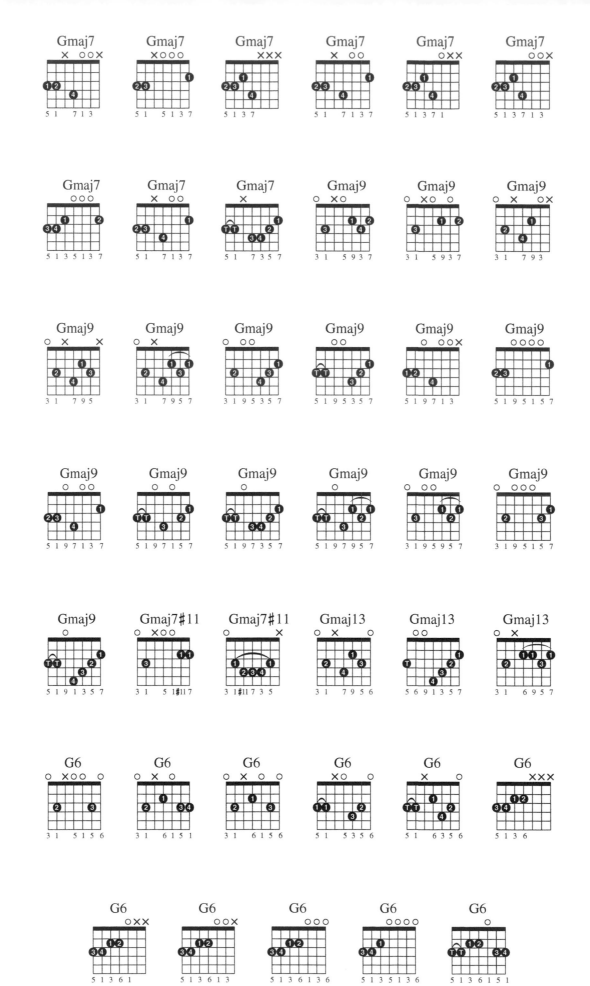

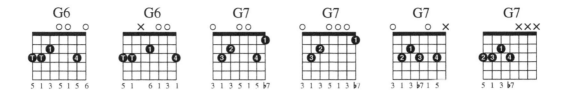

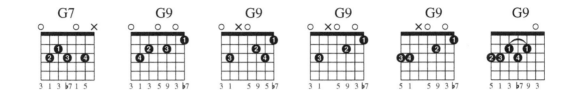

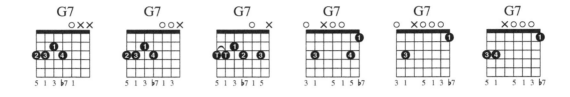

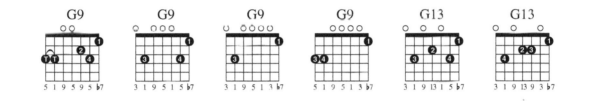

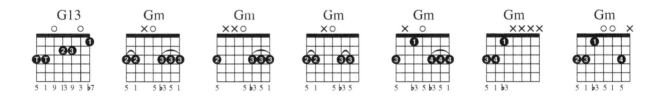

Major

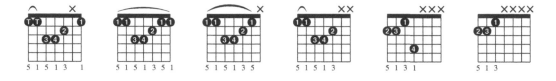

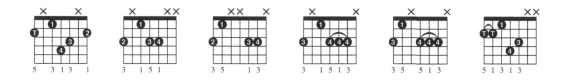

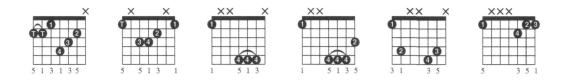

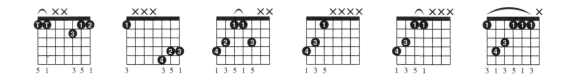

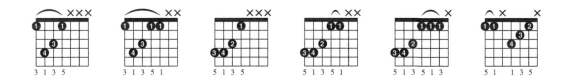

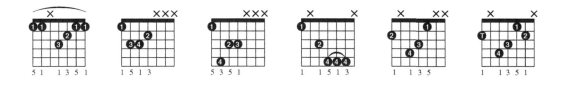

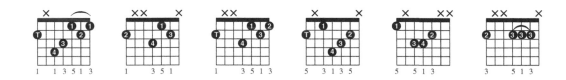

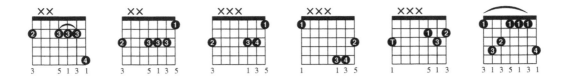

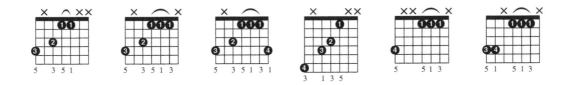

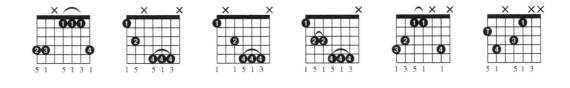

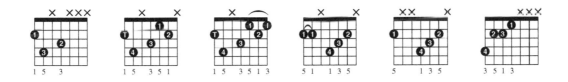

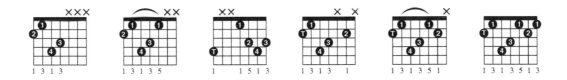

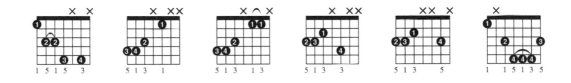

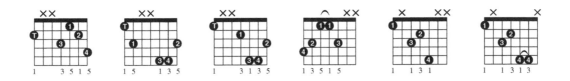

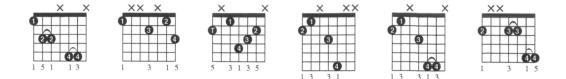

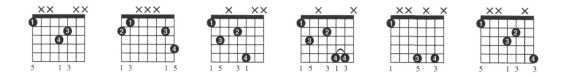

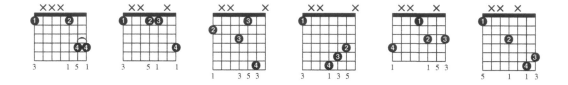

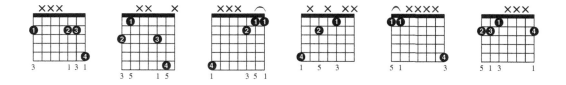

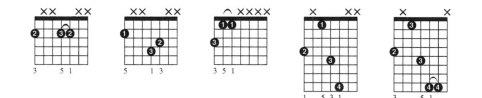

Major add9

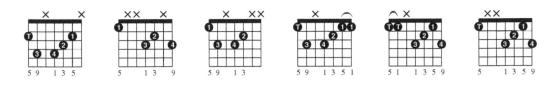

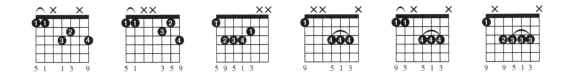

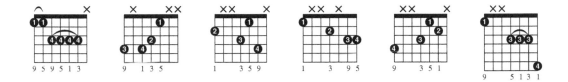

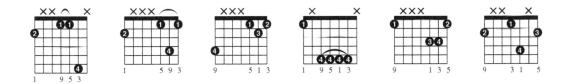

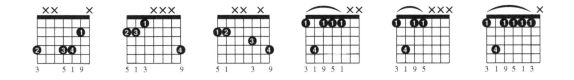

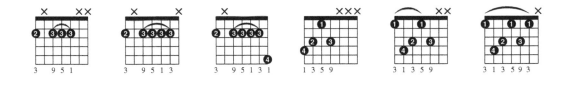

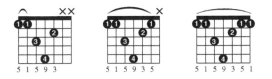

Suspended 4th

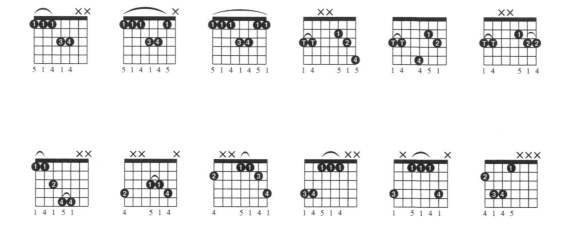

Major 6th

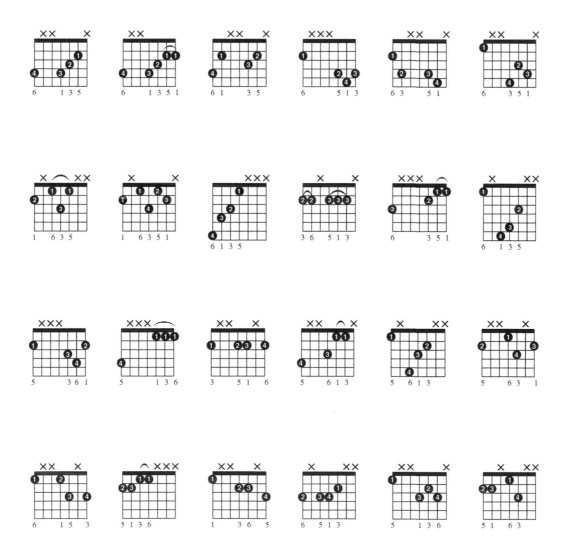

26

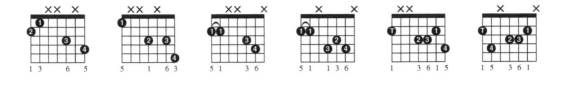

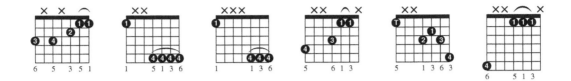

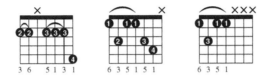

Major 7th

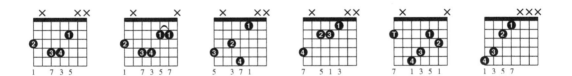

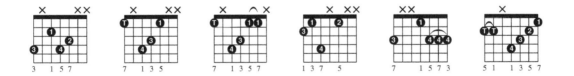

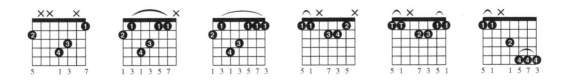

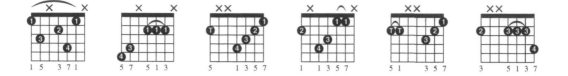

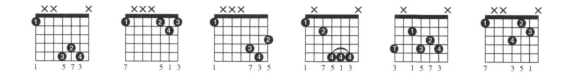

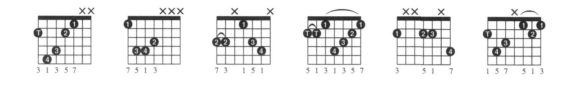

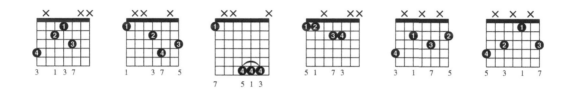

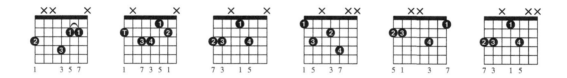

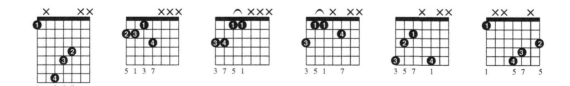

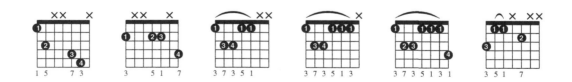

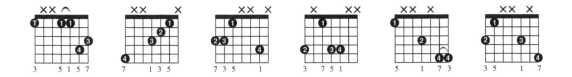

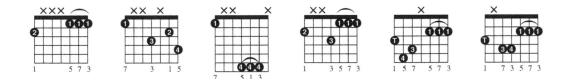

Major 9th

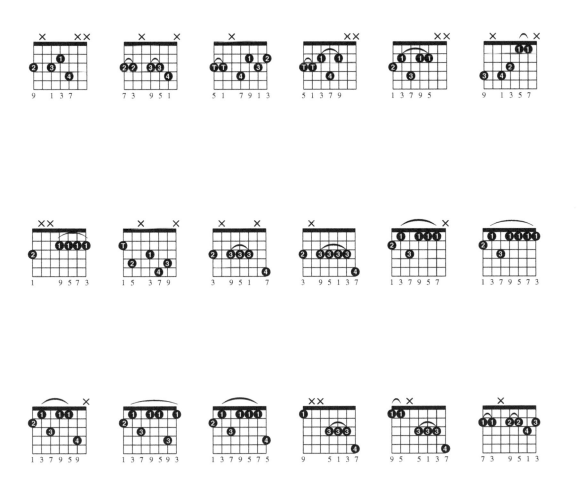

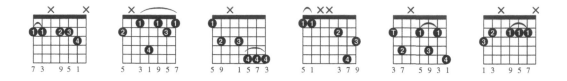

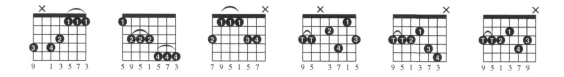

Major 7♯11

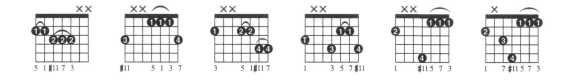

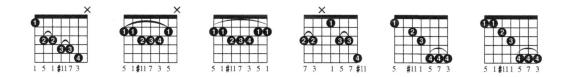

Major 13th

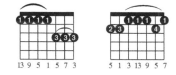

Minor

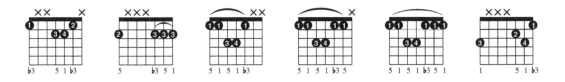

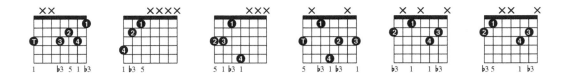

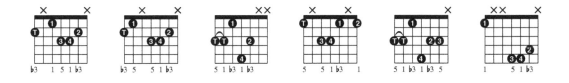

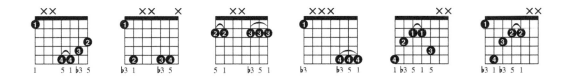

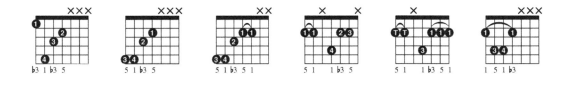

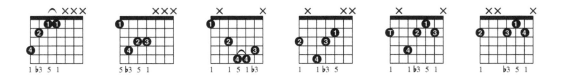

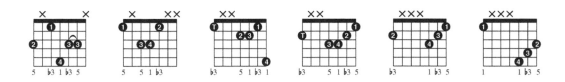

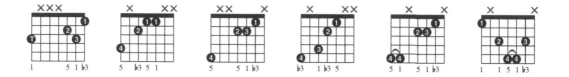

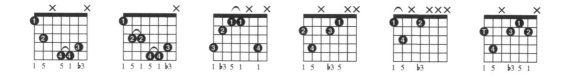

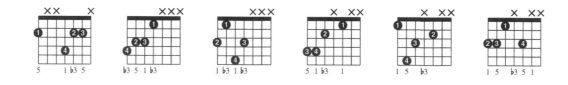

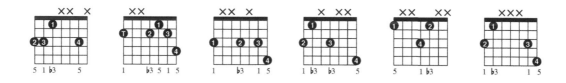

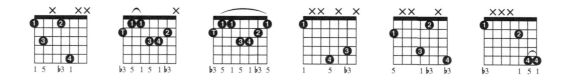

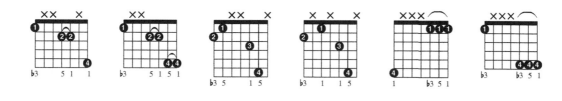

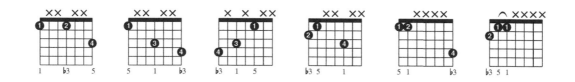

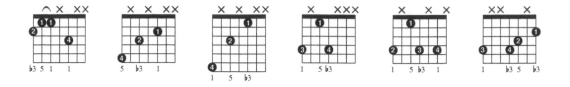

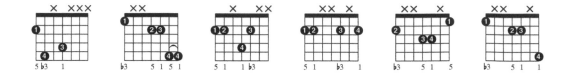

Minor add9

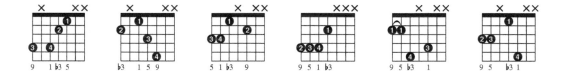

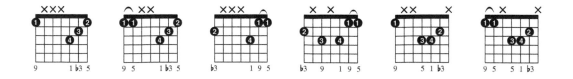

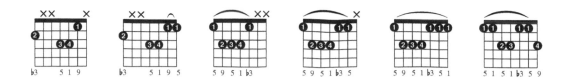

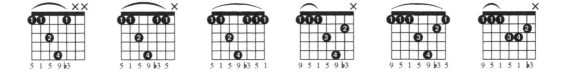

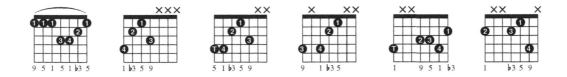

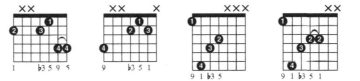

Minor 6th

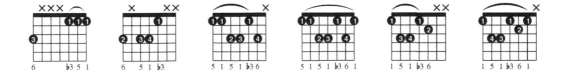

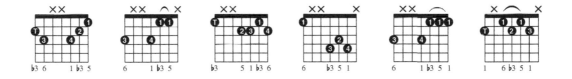

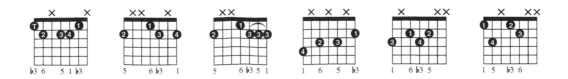

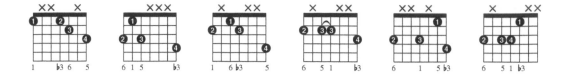

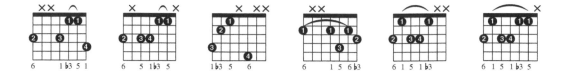

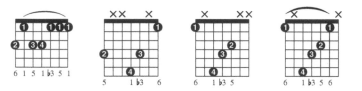

Minor 7th

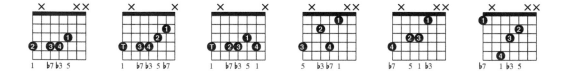

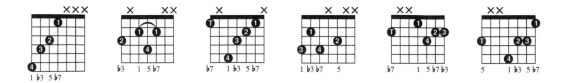

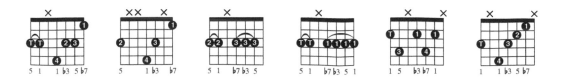

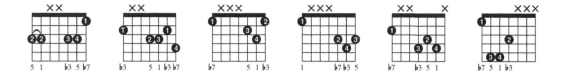

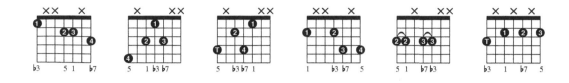

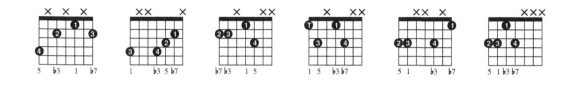

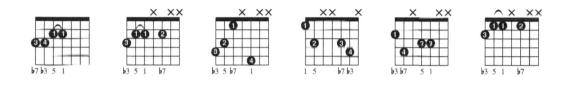

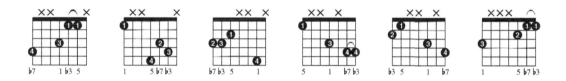

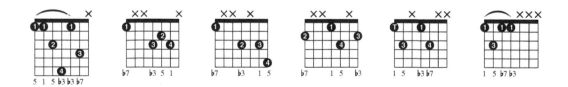

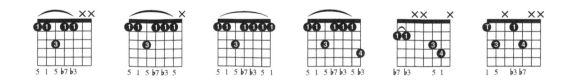

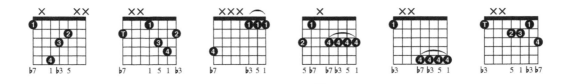

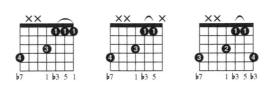

Minor 7♭5

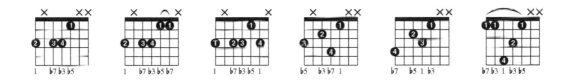

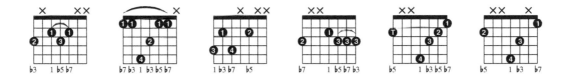

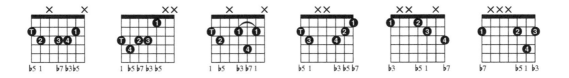

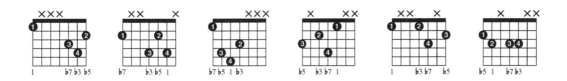

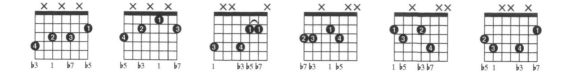

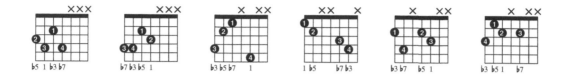

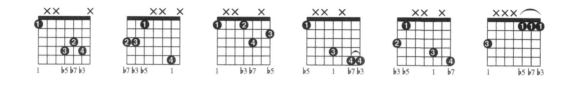

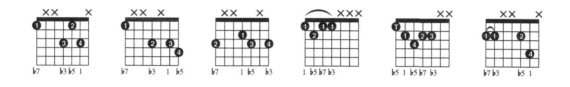

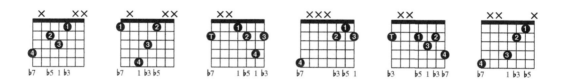

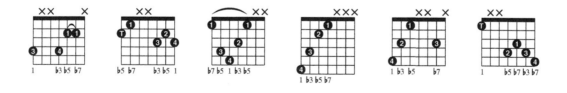

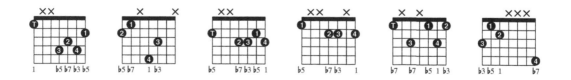

b3 b7   b5 1 b3   1 b5 b7 b3 b7   1 b5 b7 b3 b7 1   1 b5 b7 b3 b7 b3   1 b5 b7 b3 1 b5

Minor 11th

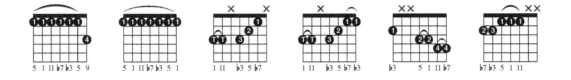

5 1 11 b7 b3 5 9   5 1 11 b7 b3 5 1   1 11 b3 5 b7   1 11 b3 5 b7 b3   b3 5 1 11 b7   b7 b3 5 1 11

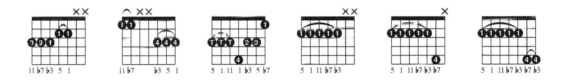

11 b7 b3 5 1   11 b7 b3 5 1   5 1 11 b3 5 b7   5 1 11 b7 b3   5 1 11 b7 b3 b7   5 1 11 b7 b3 b7 b3

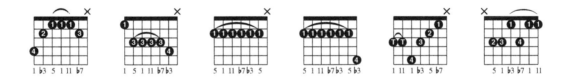

1 b3 5 1 11 b7   1 5 1 11 b7 b3   5 1 11 b7 b3 5   5 1 11 b7 b3 5 b3   1 11 1 b3 5 b7   5 1 b3 b7 1 11

5 1 11 b7 b3 5 1   11 b3 1 5 b7   b7 b3 1 11 1   5 1 11 b7 b3 1 11   5 1 11 b7 b3 5 11   b7 b3 5 1 11 11

Minor 9th

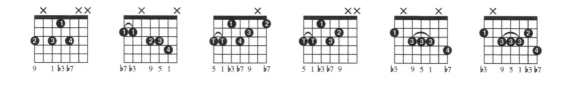

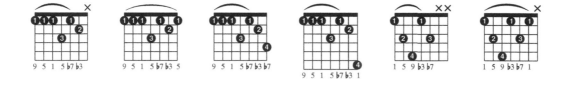

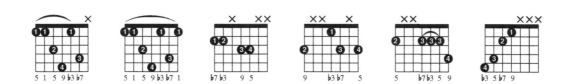

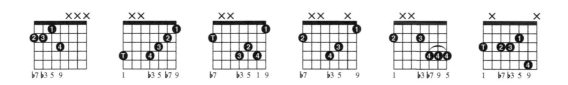

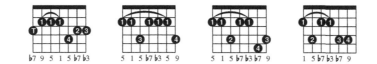

Minor, Major 7th

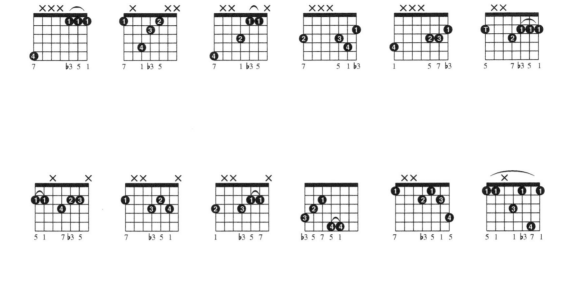

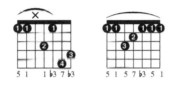

Minor 9th, Major 7th

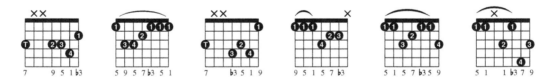

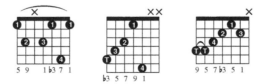

Dominant 7th

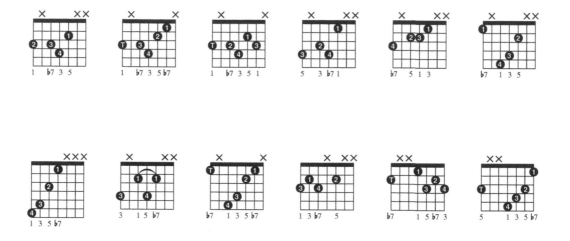

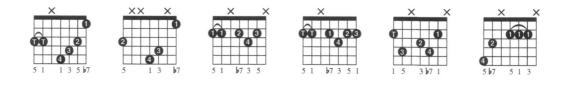

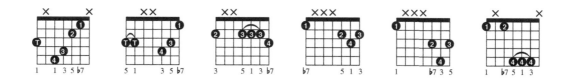

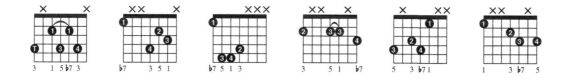

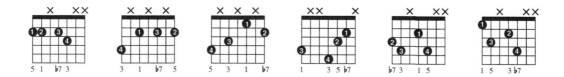

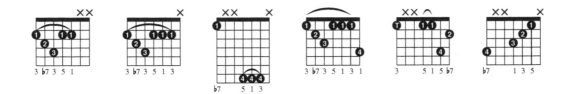

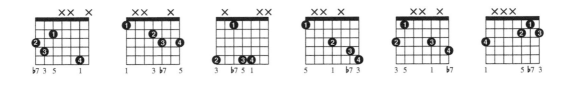

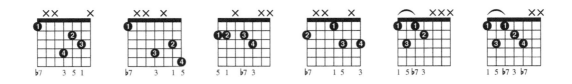

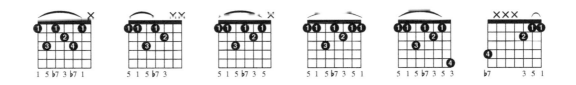

Dominant 7 sus4

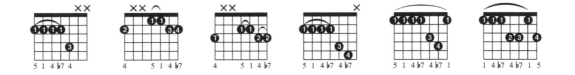

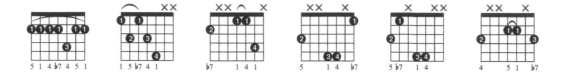

Dominant 9th

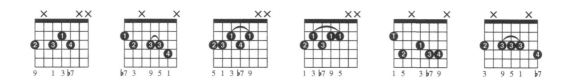

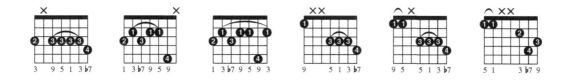

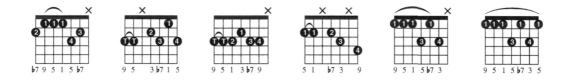

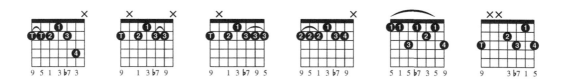

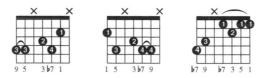

Dominant 7♯9

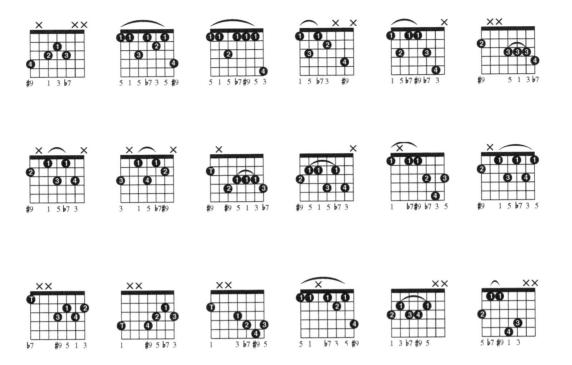

Dominant 13th

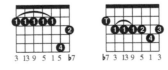

Diminished

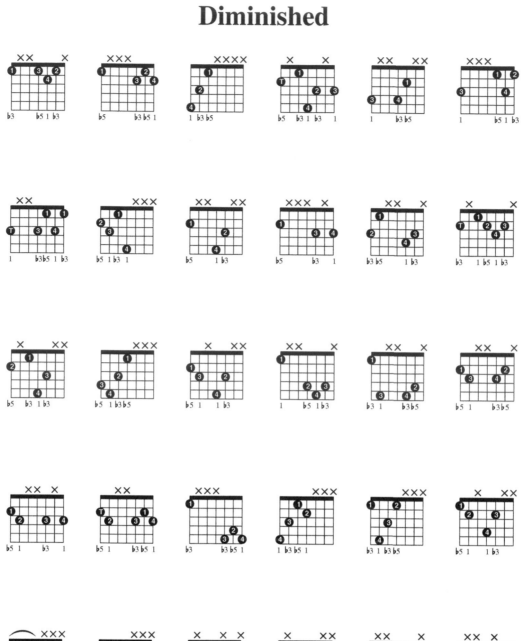

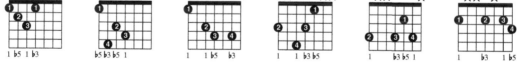

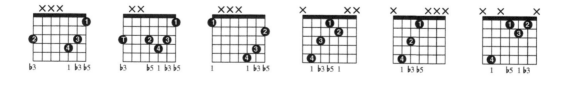

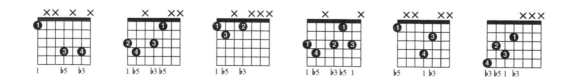

Augmented

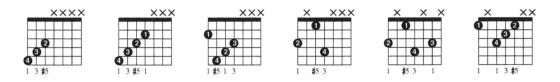

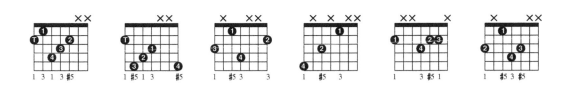

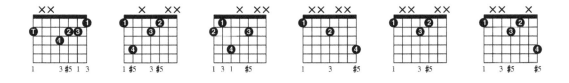

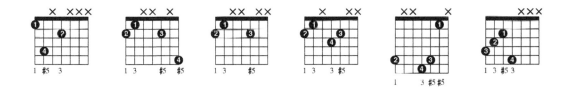

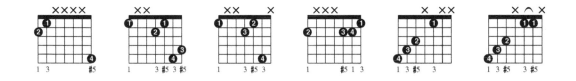

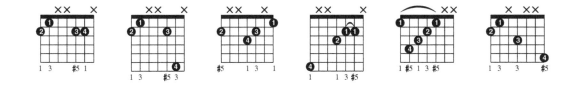

Chord Progressions

Now that you've learned a horde of new chords, you need to become comfortable playing through chord *changes* using those new forms. Here are some common chord progressions using some of my favorite chord voicings for the seven-string guitar. The top row of symbols (Roman numerals) indicates where each chord fits in the particular key. The second row contains the chord names. Beneath that is the respective chord grid and voicing.

Progression 1

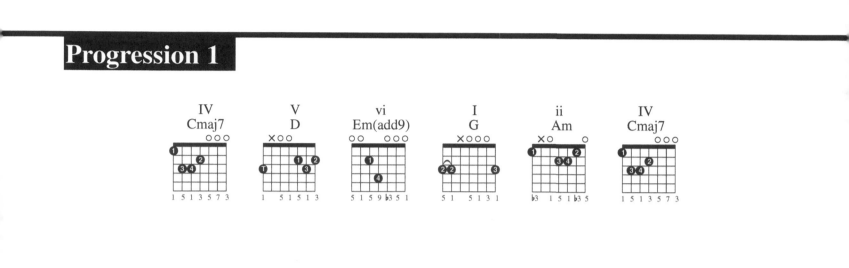

Progression 2

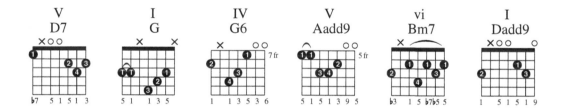

Progression 3

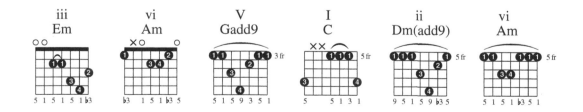

Progression 4

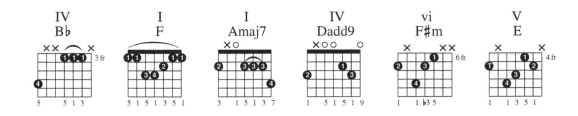

Progression 5

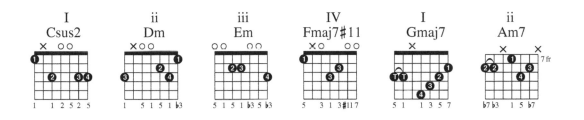

Progression 6

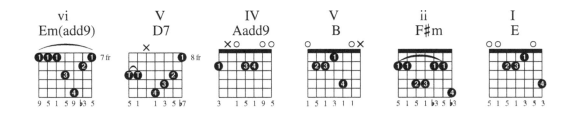

Progression 7

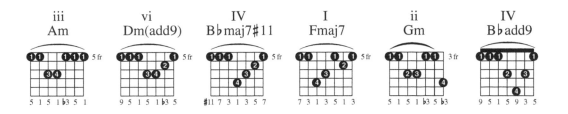

Progression 8

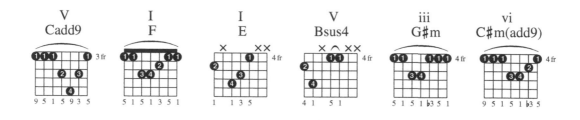

V	I	I	V	iii	vi
Cadd9	F	E	Bsus4	G#m	C#m(add9)

Progression 9

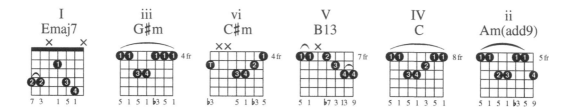

I	iii	vi	V	IV	ii
Emaj7	G#m	C#m	B13	C	Am(add9)

Progression 10

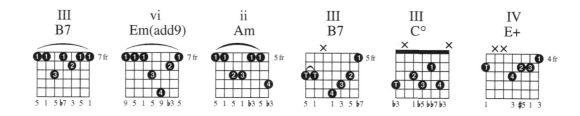

III	vi	ii	III	III	IV
B7	Em(add9)	Am	B7	C°	E+

Arpeggios

Many great guitarists like Chuck Wayne, Frank Gambale, Yngwie Malmsteen, Paul Gilbert, and Steve Vai, as well as the famous violinist Niccolo Paganini, are known for their amazing arpeggio techniques. If you're already familiar with playing arpeggios on a six-string guitar, this chapter will not only help you become comfortable and confident adding notes from the low B string to your current repertoire of arpeggios, it will also introduce you to several new patterns as well.

Arpeggios are chord tones played separately but in succession. Rather than plucking or strumming the chord, play each note of the chord in the order it appears on the fingerboard—one at a time. There are many picking techniques you can use with arpeggios. You can use alternate picking, double- or triple-pick every note, or perhaps the most popular and impressive technique: *sweep picking*. Sweep picking is performed based on the physical layout of the notes on the fretboard. Anytime you're required to physically move your hand toward the floor (from low to high pitches), use a downstroke for each attack. Conversely, when you're moving your pick hand toward your head (from high to low pitches), use an upstroke for each attack. The concept is very closely related to strumming, however, the difference lies in muting each string after the note has been struck, rather than letting it ring out. This muting is performed by the fretting hand. The arpeggio shapes should not be fretted as a chord, but rather one note at a time so the notes don't ring together.

Always practice with a metronome, and start practicing slowly and evenly for a few reasons:
1. It will greatly improve your timing and technique.
2. You can monitor your progress by increasing the tempo, or beats per minute (bpm).
3. By practicing slowly, evenly, and in time, you will notice that when you play at faster tempos your technique will be much cleaner and precise.

In this chapter you will be learning the following arpeggios:

- Major (1–3–5)
- Minor (1–♭3–5)
- Diminished (1–♭3–♭5)
- Major 7th (1–3–5–7)
- Minor 7th (1–♭3–5–♭7)
- Minor 7♭5 (1–♭3–♭5–♭7)
- Dominant 7th (1–3–5–♭7)

Each arpeggio is presented on a grid, with the recommended fingering appearing in the dots on the grid, in the same manner as the chords were presented earlier. Since there may be more than one note per string, however, you will notice that some strings will have stacked intervals beneath the grid. The order of the intervals simply follows the order of the notes on the string.

Just as the chords in this book are movable forms, so too are the arpeggios presented here. To determine the root, simply find an interval labeled "1," and match it to that fret's note. So, if interval 1 of a major arpeggio appears on the 7th fret of the 6th string (B note), the arpeggio is B major (see example below).

Major

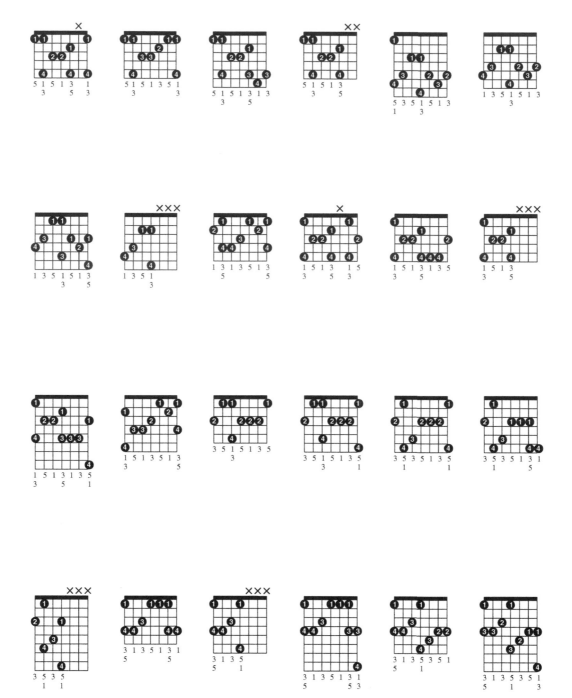

Minor

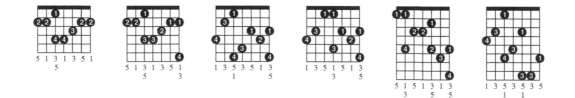

54

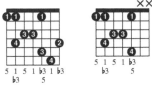
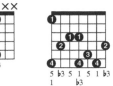

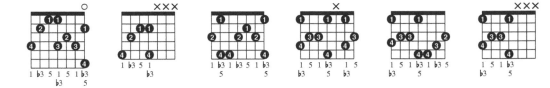
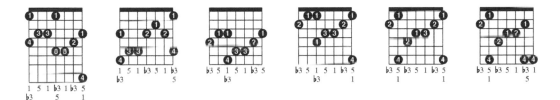

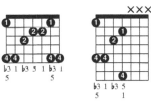

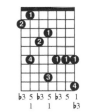

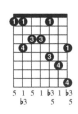
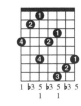

Diminished

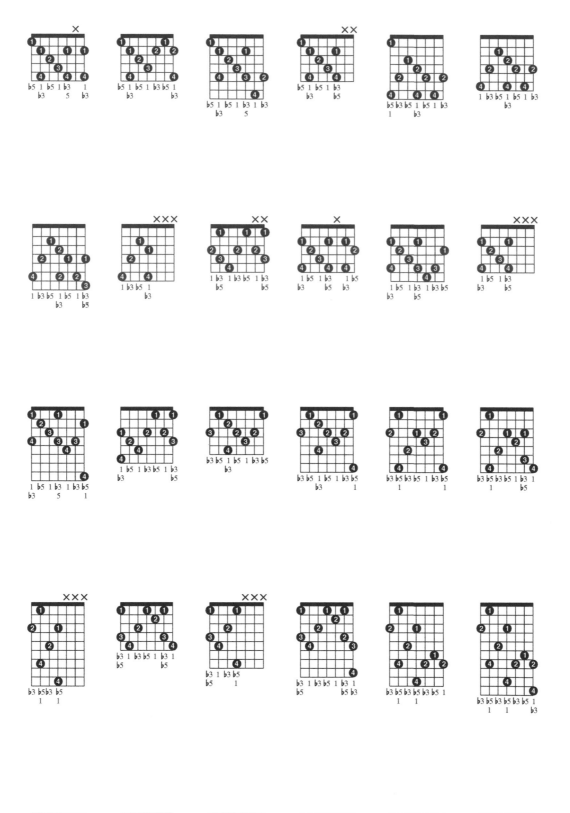

Major 7th

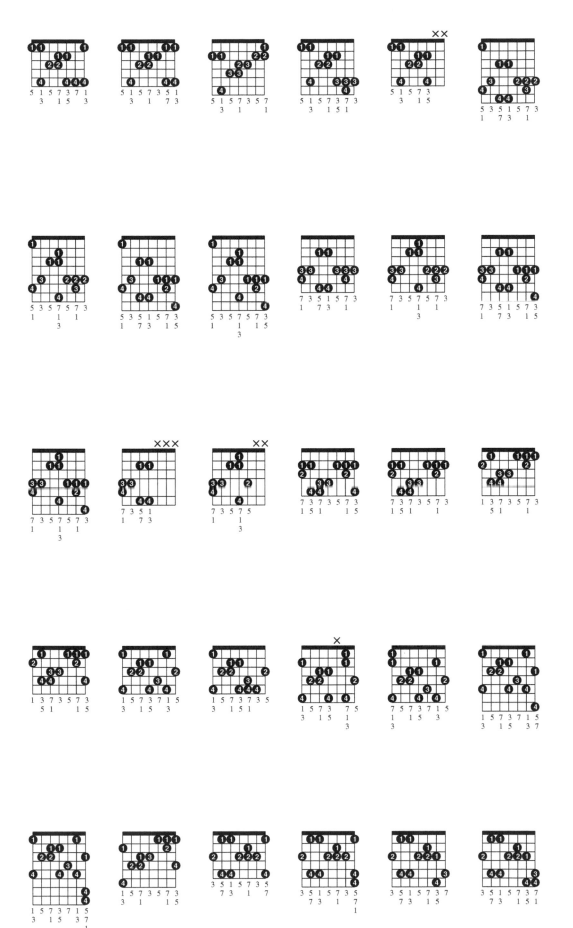

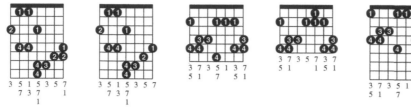
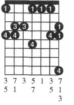

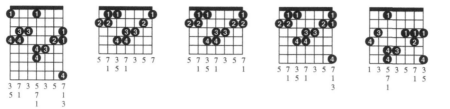

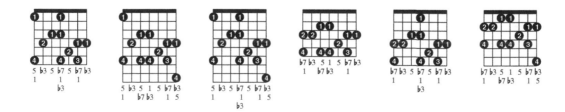

Minor 7th

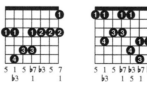
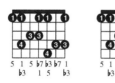
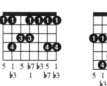
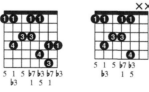

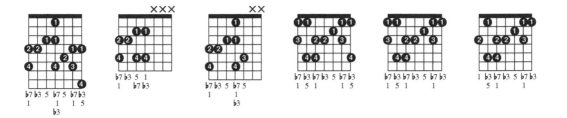

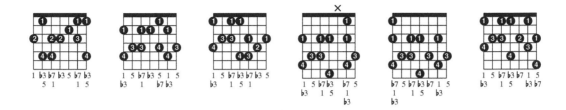

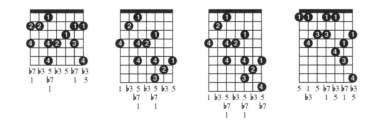

Minor 7♭5

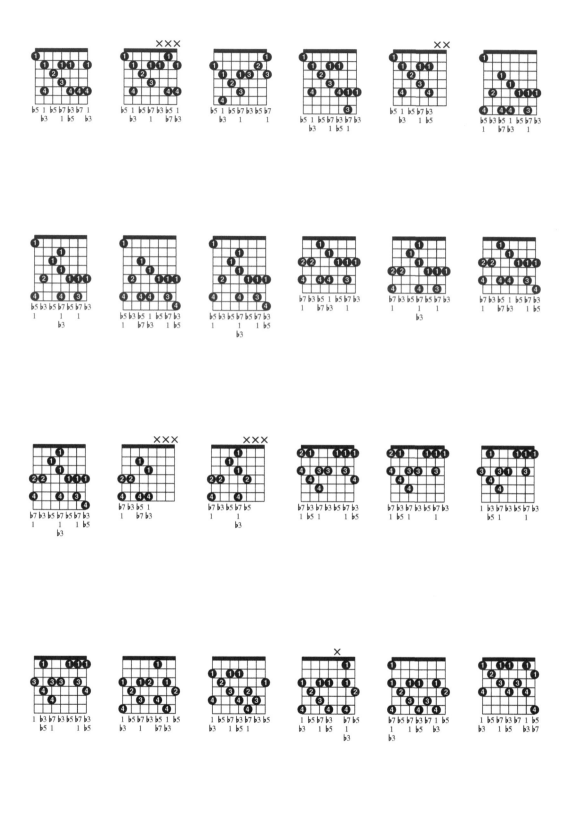

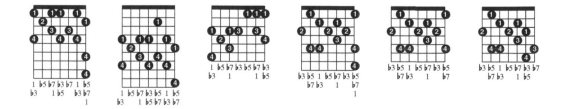

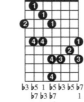
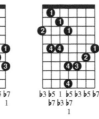

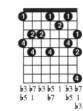

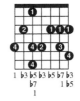

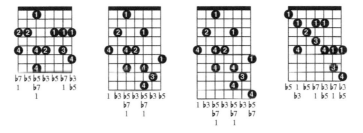

Dominant 7th

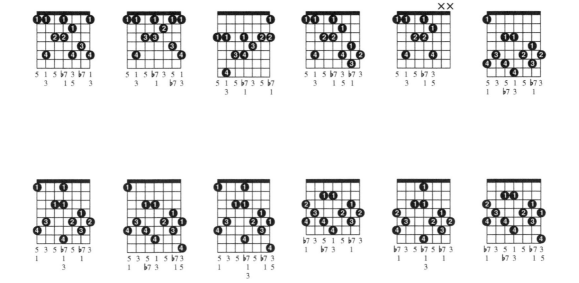

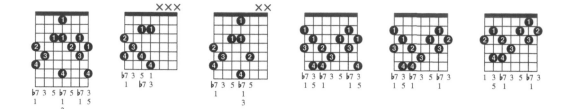

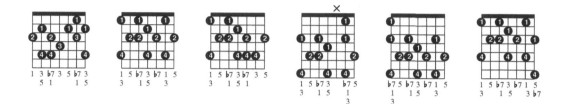

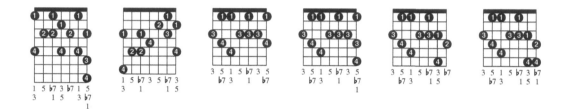

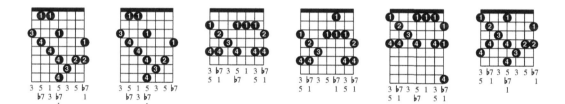

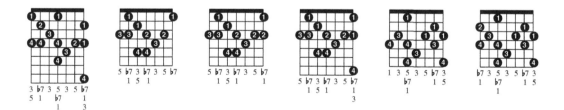

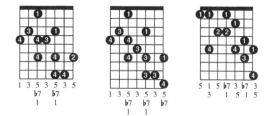

Pentatonic Scales

Pentatonic means literally "five tones," so a pentatonic scale contains five notes. There are two primary types of pentatonic scale: major and minor. The major pentatonic scale is simply the major scale with the 4th and 7th degrees omitted (1–2–3–5–6). This scale can be used anytime you're improvising over a major chord. It is quite common in pop and country music. The minor pentatonic scale is simply the natural minor scale with the 2nd and 6th degrees omitted (1–♭3–4–5–♭7). This scale can be used over minor chords, and is commonly heard in blues and rock music.

The pentatonic scale is a very "user-friendly" scale, but with this label comes a caveat: In all of your pentatonic applications, you must resolve all colors religiously. Let your ear be your guide, as your aural sensibility combined with your knowledge of theory and harmony will let you know whether the note you just played is at conflict with or in perfect harmony with the underlying chord structure.

In this chapter, you learn five positions for both the major and minor pentatonic scales. The positions are determined by the scale degree on which the pattern begins:

	Major Pentatonic	**Minor Pentatonic**
Position 1:	1–2–3–5–6	1–♭3–4–5–♭7
Position 2:	2–3–5–6–1	♭3–4–5–♭7–1
Position 3:	3–5–6–1–2	4–5–♭7–1–♭3
Position 4:	5–6–1–2–3	5–♭7–1–♭3–4
Position 5:	6–1–2–3–5	♭7–1–♭3–4-5

As you can see, each position contains the same scale degrees; they just begin on a different note. Using C major pentatonic as an example, the notes for position 1 are: C–D–E–G–A. Position 2 begins on the second degree of the scale: D–E–G–A–C. In the language of music theory, these positions represent *modes* of the pentatonic scale. (We'll further discuss modes in the next chapter.) One of the cool things about these modes, or positions, is that they all interconnect on the fretboard, allowing you to play notes from the pentatonic scales (or any scale) *anywhere* on the neck.

Each position for both the major and minor pentatonic scales is presented here in grid form, in the same manner as the chords and arpeggios from the preceding chapters. Again, to find the root of the scale (and thus its name), simply locate the note that corresponds to the interval labeled "1" beneath the grid.

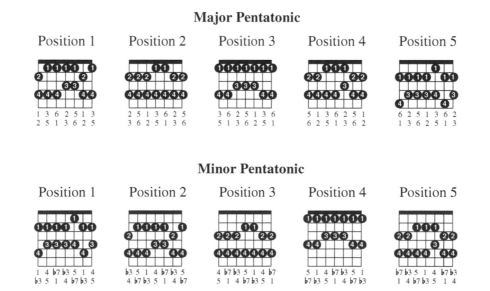

E Phrygian

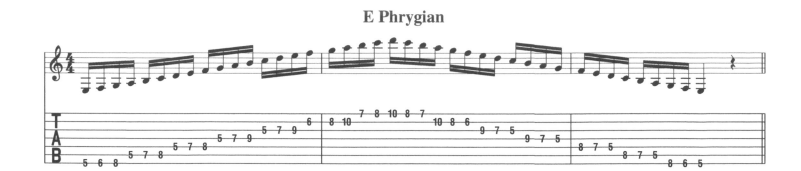

F Lydian

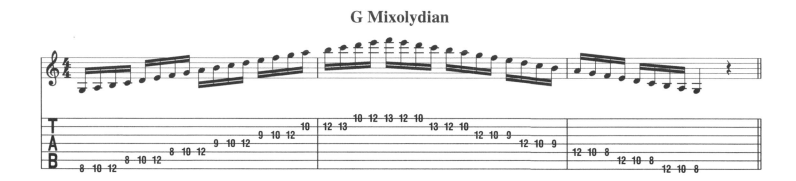

G Mixolydian

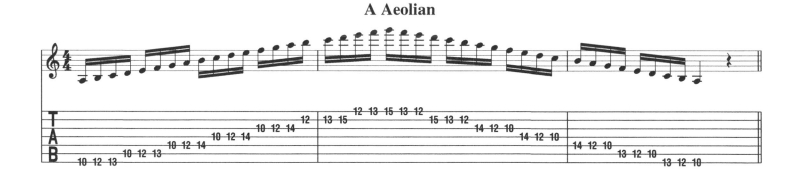

A Aeolian

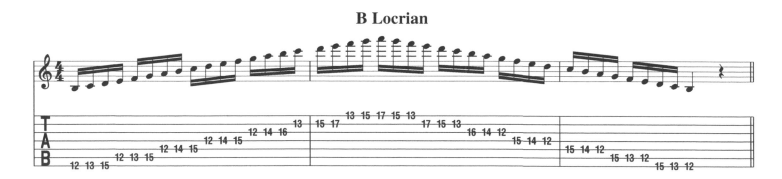

B Locrian

D♭ Major

D♭ Ionian

E♭ Dorian

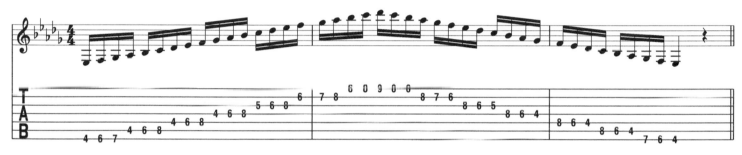

F Phrygian

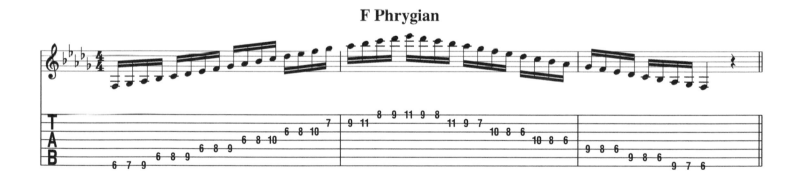

G♭ Lydian

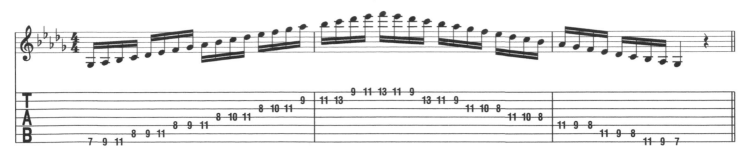

A♭ Mixolydian

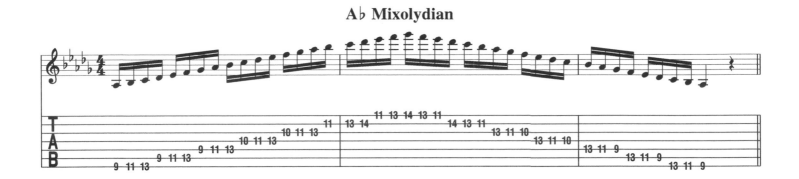

B♭ Aeolian

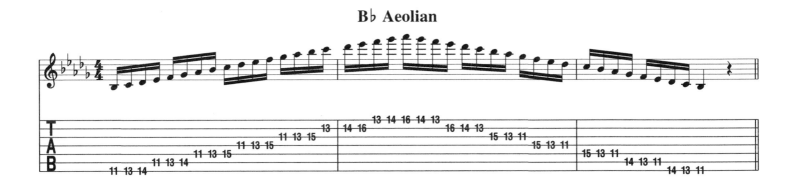

C Locrian

D Major

D Ionian

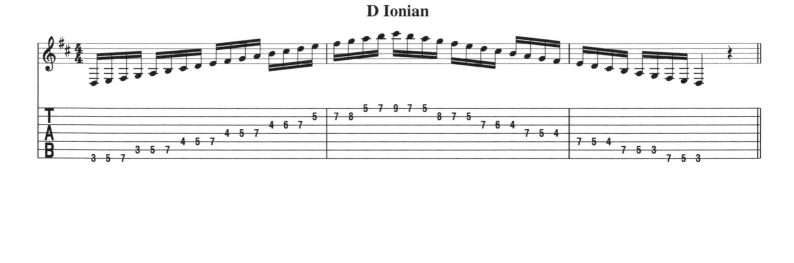

E Dorian

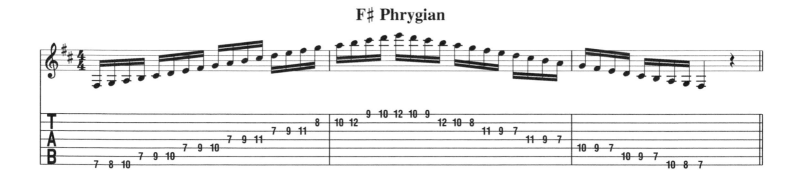

F# Phrygian

G Lydian

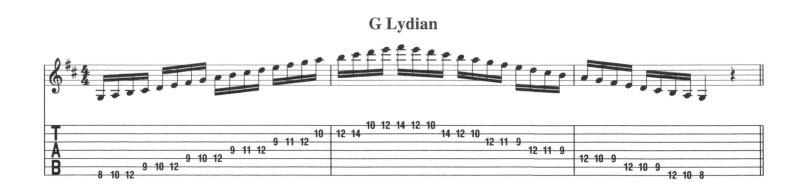

A Mixolydian

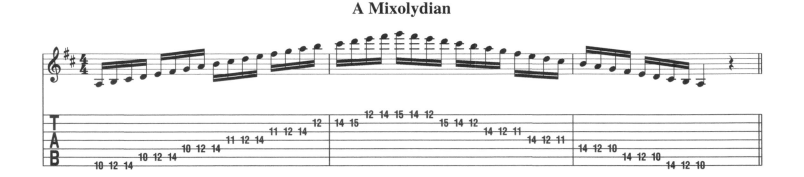

B Aeolian

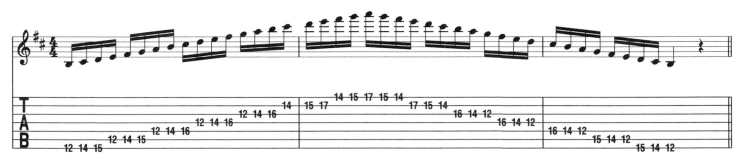

C# Locrian

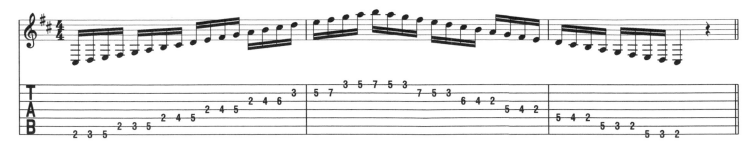

E♭ Major

E♭ Ionian

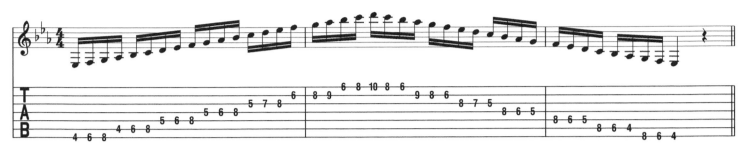

F Dorian

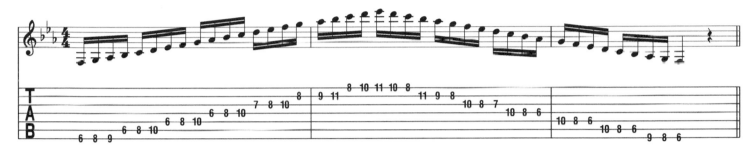

G Phrygian

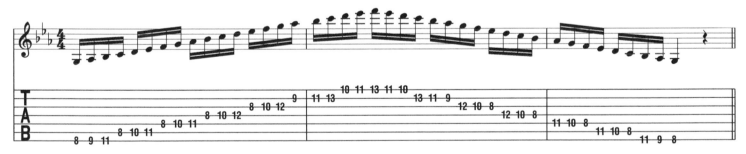

Ab Lydian

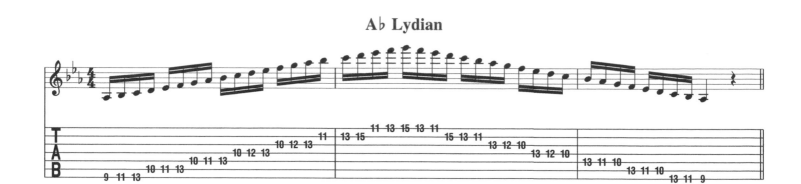

Bb Mixolydian

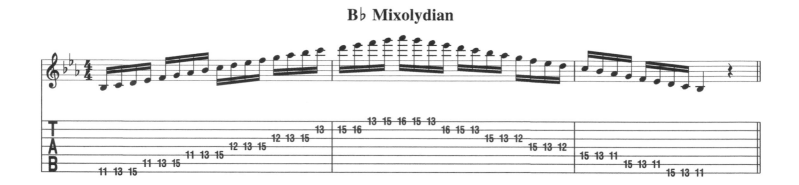

C Aeolian

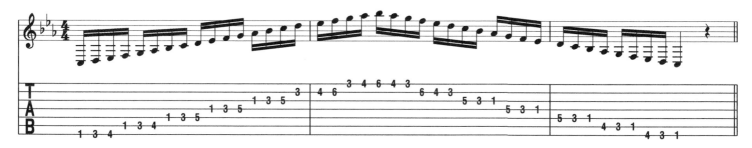

D Locrian

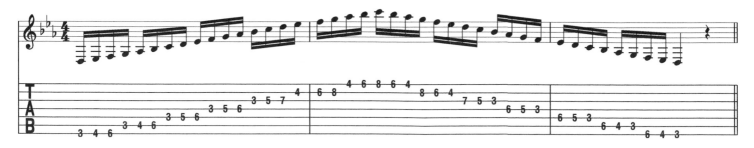

E Major

E Ionian

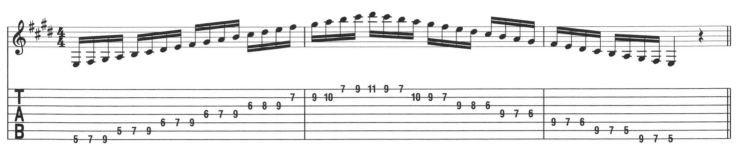

F♯ Dorian

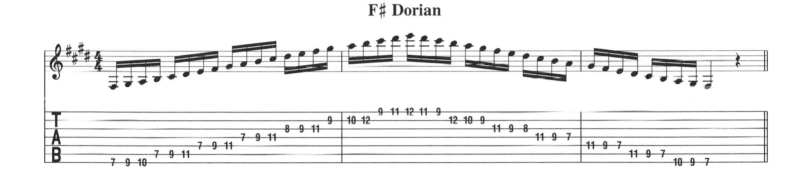

G♯ Phrygian

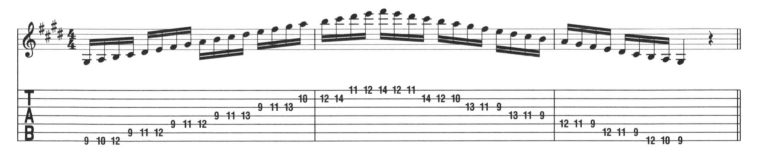

A Lydian

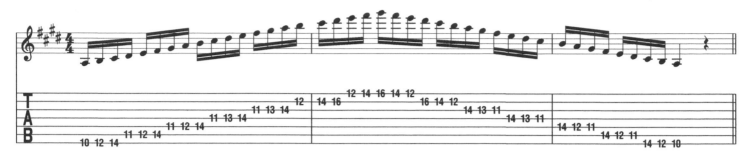

B Mixolydian

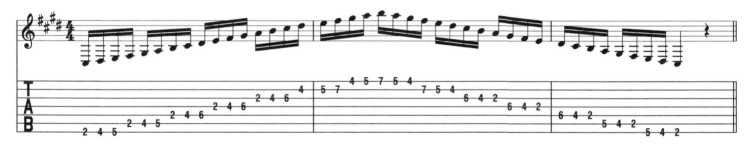

C# Aeolian

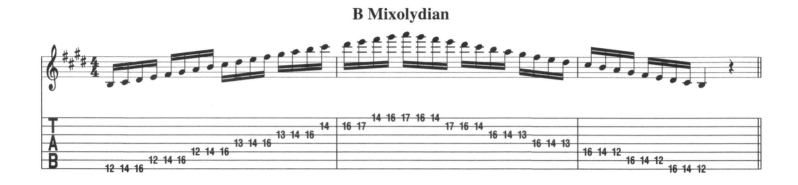

D# Locrian

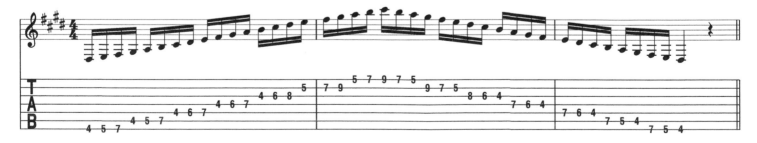

F Major

F Ionian

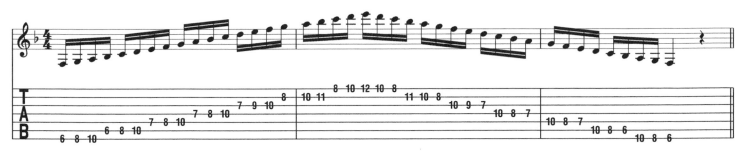

G Dorian

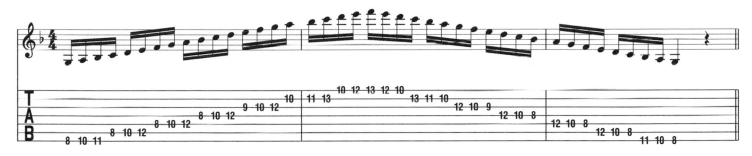

A Phrygian

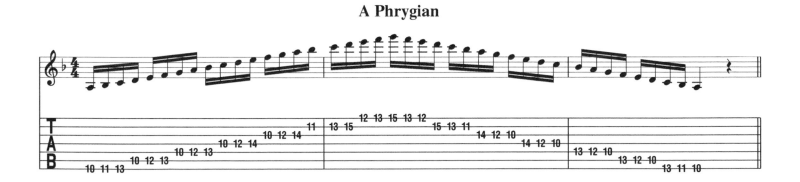

Bb Lydian

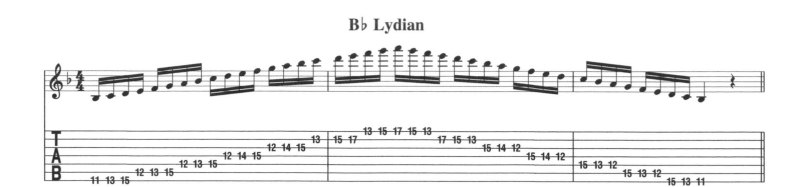

C Mixolydian

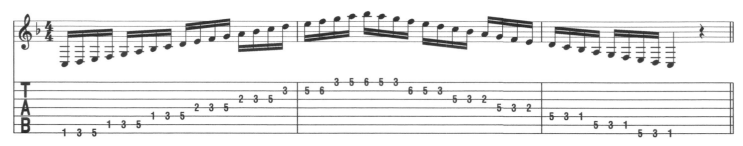

D Aeolian

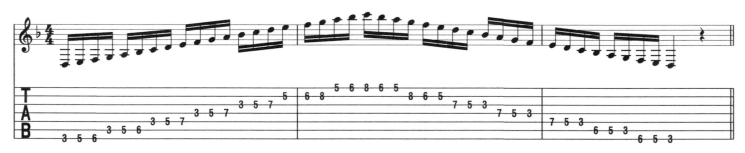

E Locrian

G♭ Major

G♭ Ionian

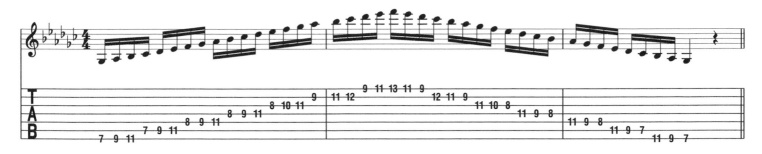

A♭ Dorian

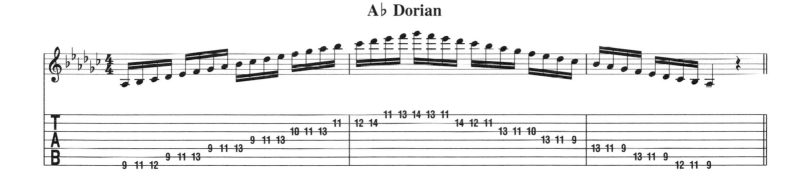

B♭ Phrygian

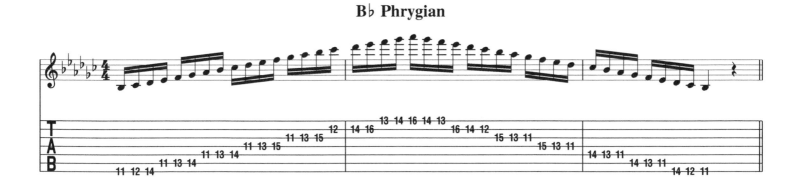

Cb Lydian

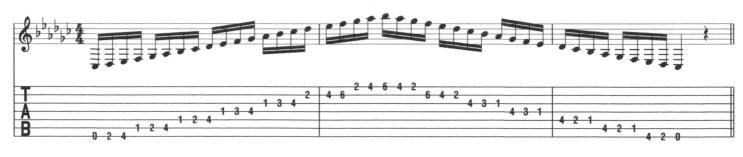

Db Mixolydian

Eb Aeolian

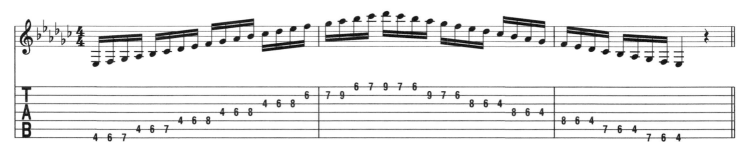

F Locrian

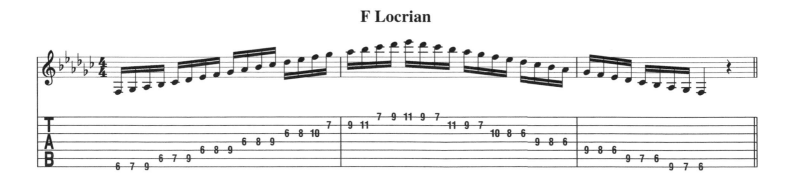

G Major

G Ionian

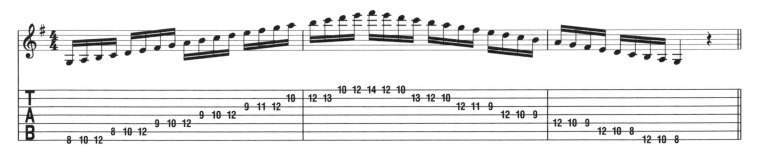

A Dorian

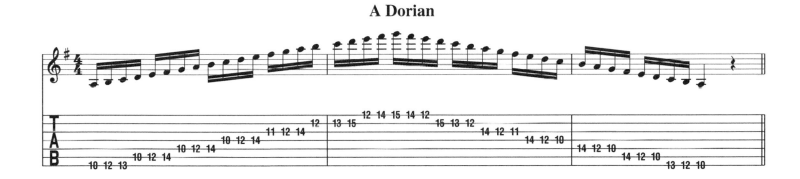

B Pyrygian

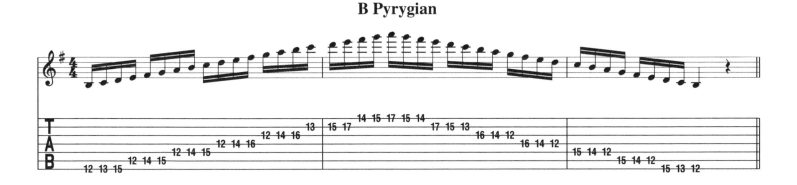

C Lydian

D Mixolydian

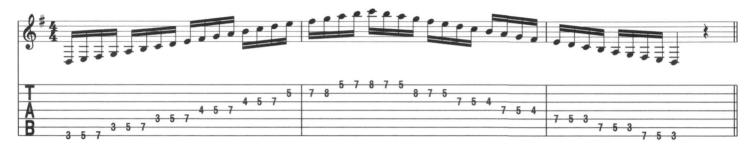

E Aeolian

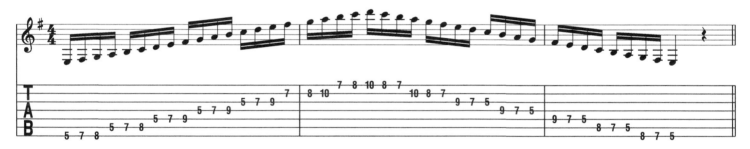

F♯ Locrian

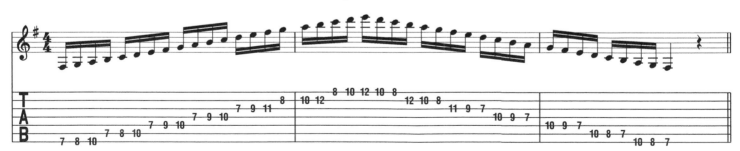

A♭ Major

A♭ Ionian

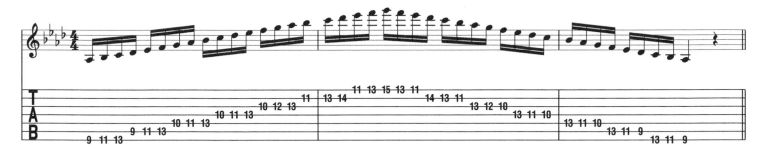

B♭ Dorian

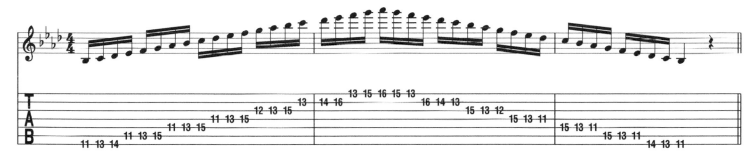

C Phrygian

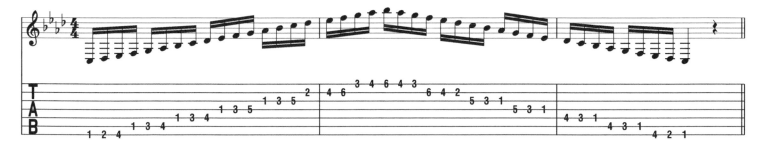

D♭ Lydian

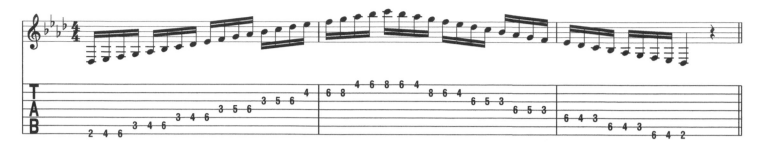

E♭ Mixolydian

F Aeolian

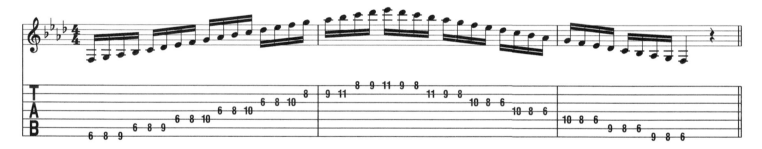

G Locrian

A Major

A Ionian

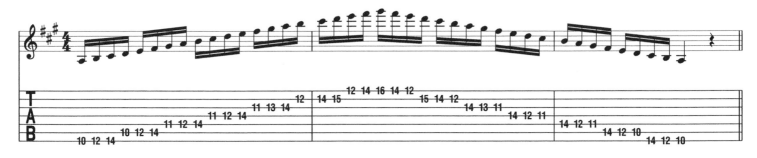

B Dorian

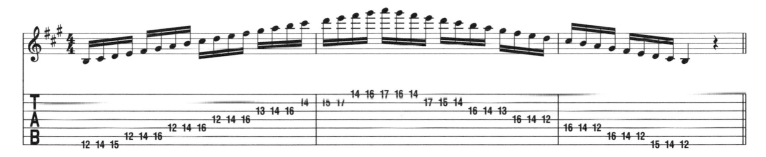

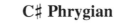

C♯ Phrygian

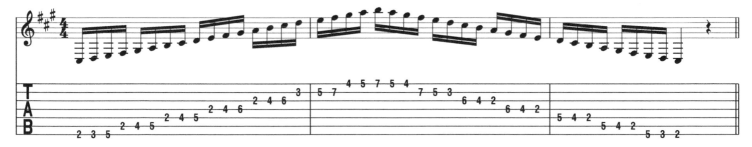

D Lydian

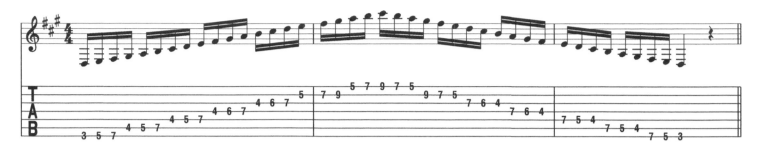

E Mixolydian

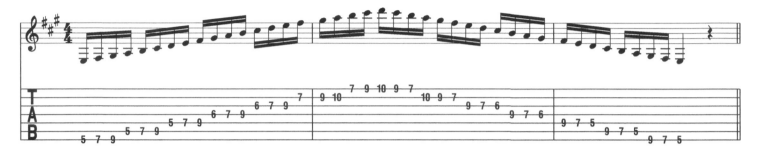

F♯ Aeolian

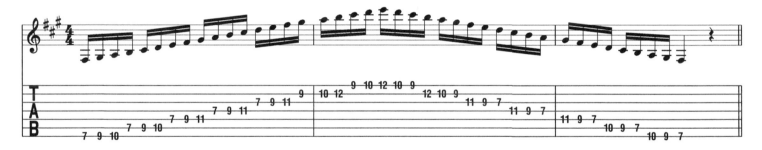

G♯ Locrian

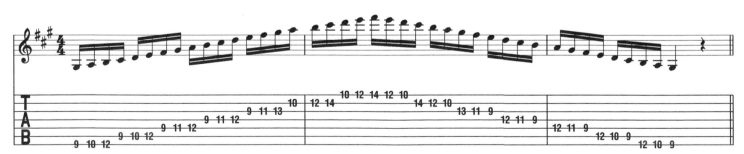

Bb Major

Bb Ionian

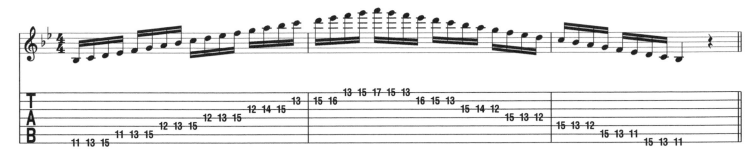

C Dorian

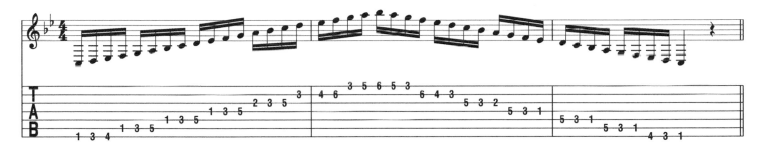

D Phrygian

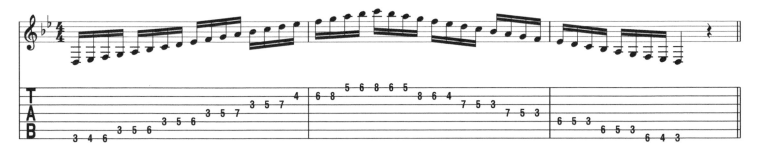

Eb Lydian

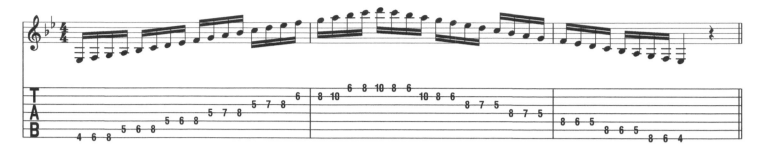

F Mixolydian

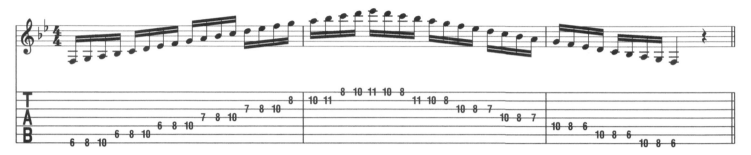

G Aeolian

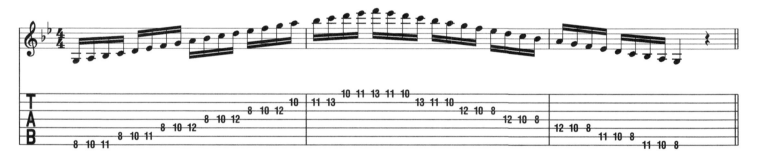

A Locrian

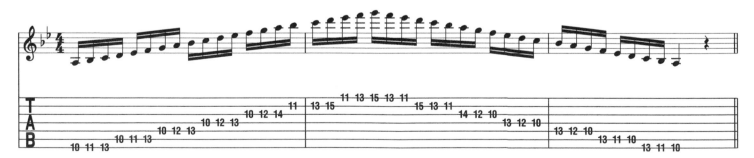

B Major

B Ionian

C# Dorian

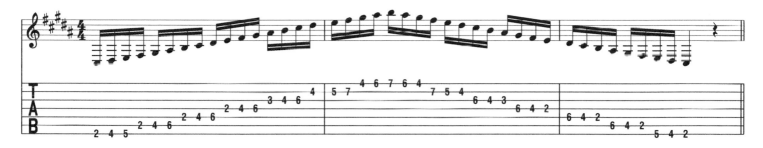

D# Phrygian

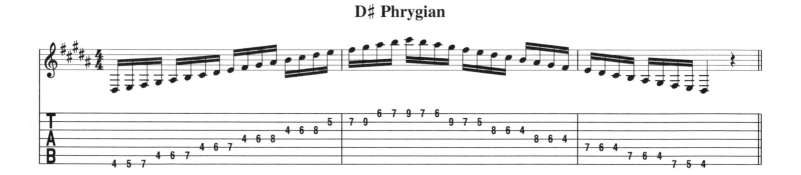

E Lydian

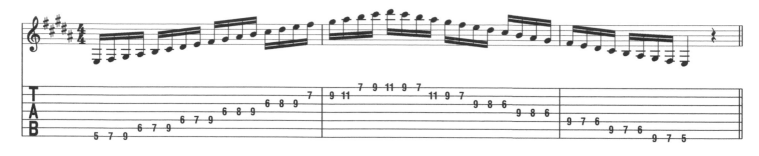

F# Mixolydian

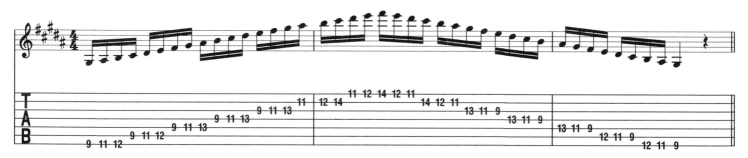

G# Aeolian

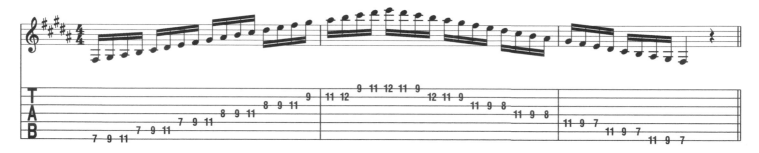

A# Locrian

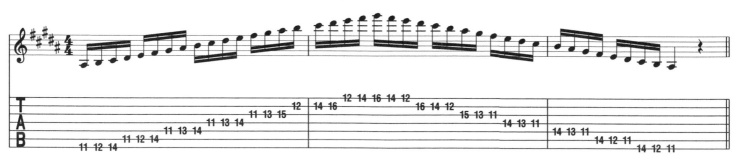

Riffs and Licks

This last chapter provides you with riffs, licks and chord progressions that build off the chord inversions, arpeggios, and scales contained in this book. Many different styles of playing are covered in these riffs and licks, and I recommend that you try them all. You may find yourself playing something that you're not familiar with and thoroughly enjoy it.

As you play through these riffs and licks, try coming up with your own ideas as well. Try new progressions and melodic ideas, but remember that, sometimes, less is more in songwriting. Let your guitar become the vocals; make it cry, talk, sing, or scream. Build the composition to a climax with movement, musical expression, and harmonic content. Don't be afraid to remove parts from a song, or to put new parts in and then change things around. Experiment with your music, your mind, and your ears. Songwriting is an art; the more you compose, the better you'll be.

Fig. 1

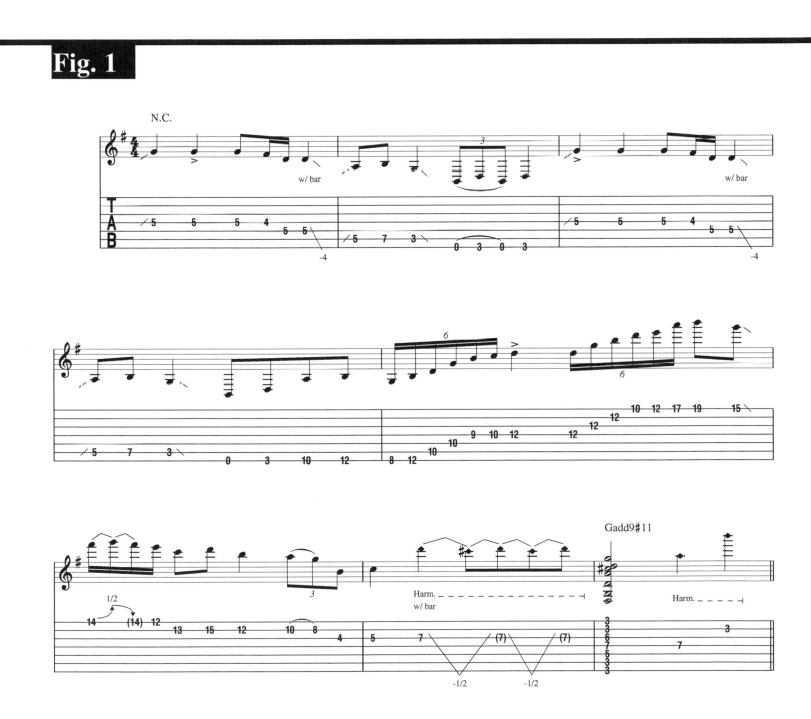

Fig. 2

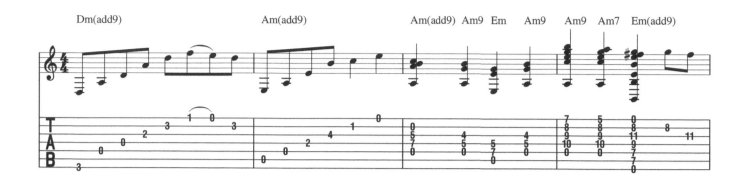

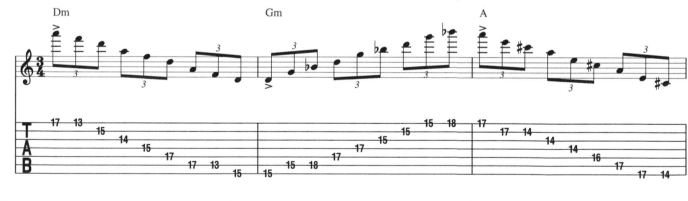

Fig. 3

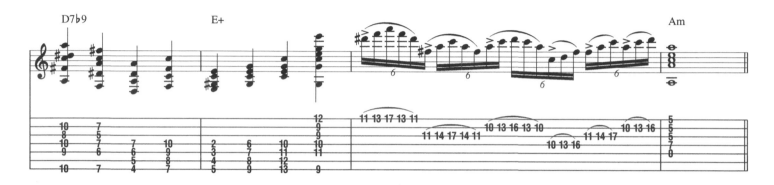

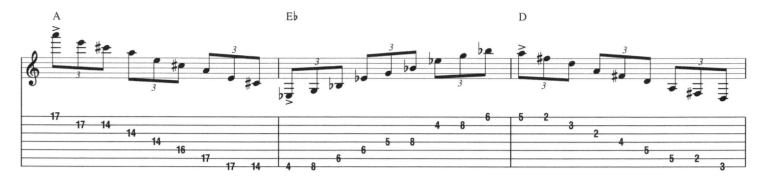

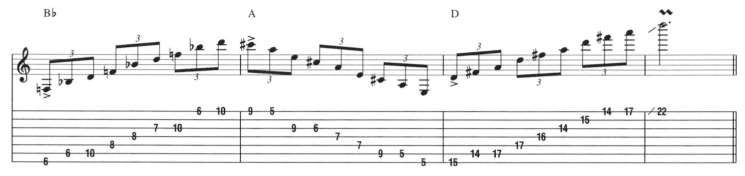

Fig. 4

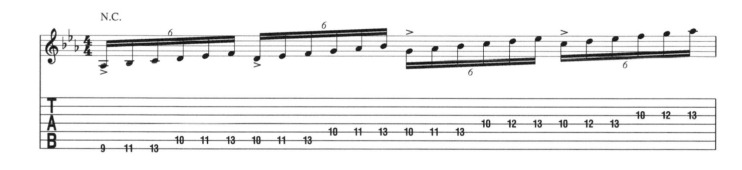

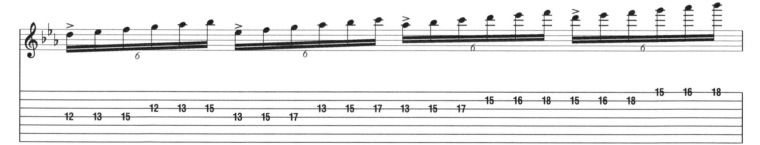

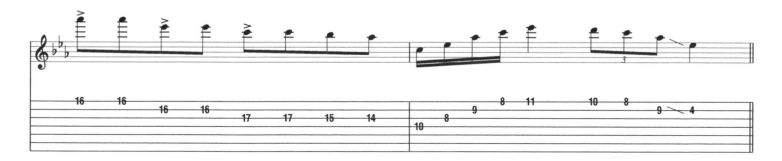

Fig. 5

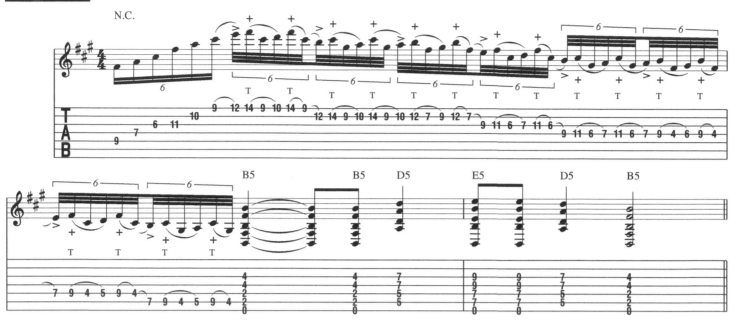

Fig. 6

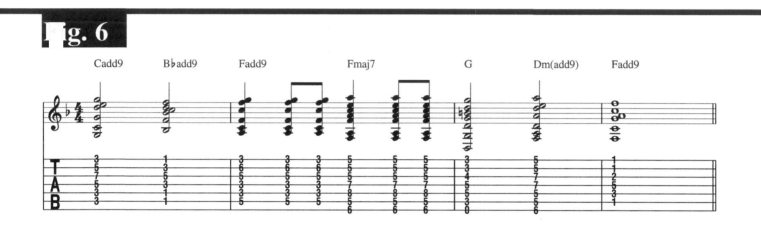

Fig. 7

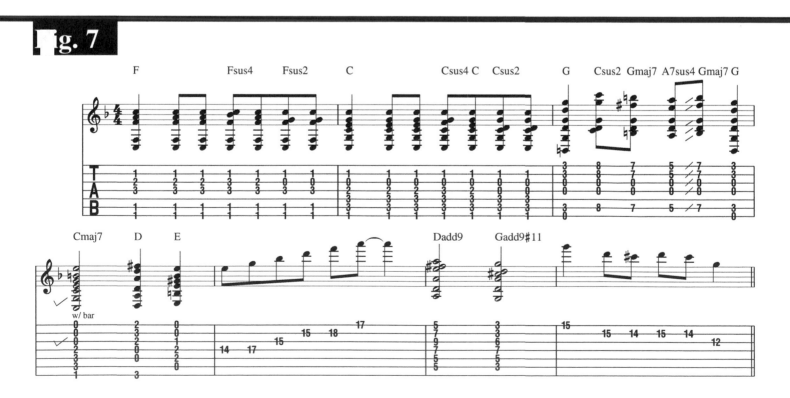

Fig. 8

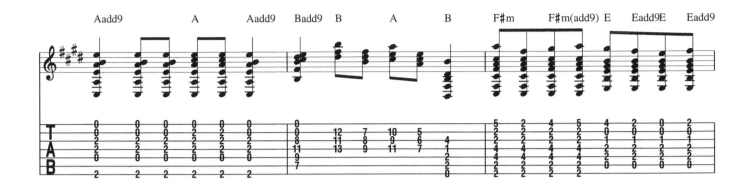

Fig. 9

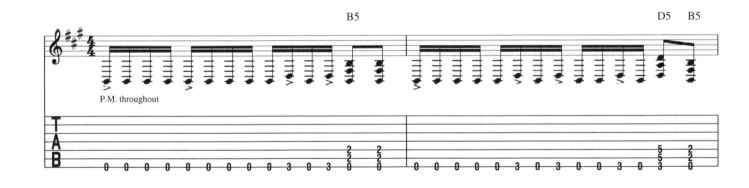

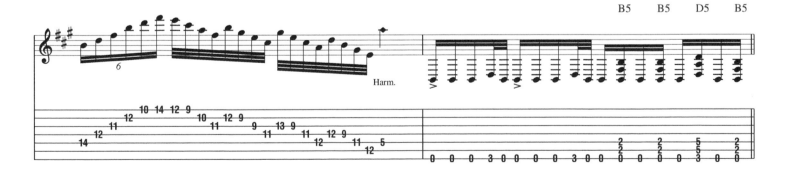

Fig. 10

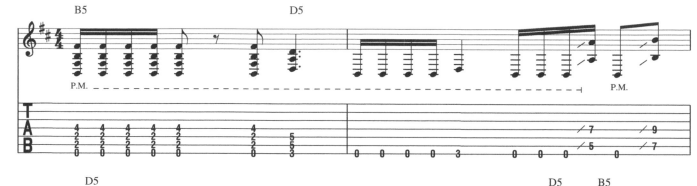

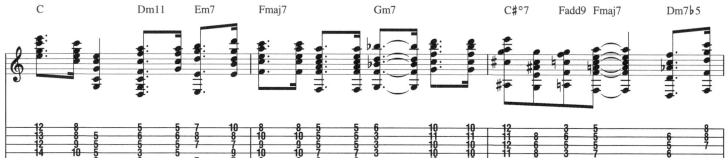

Fig. 11

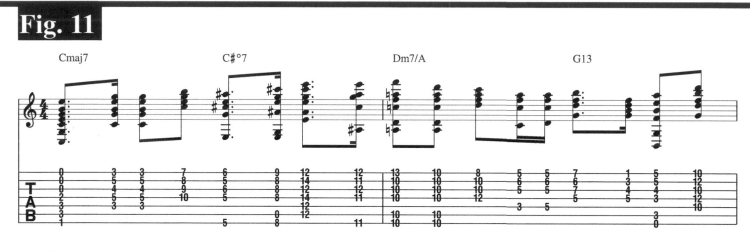

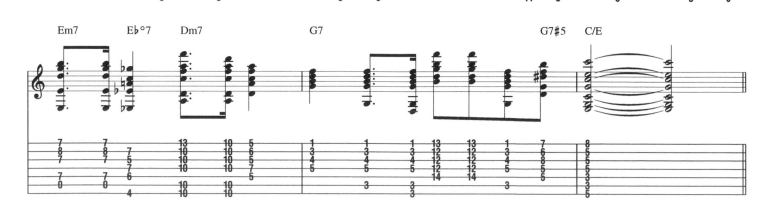

Guitar Notation Legend

Guitar Music can be notated three different ways: on a *musical staff*, in *tablature*, and in *rhythm slashes*.

RHYTHM SLASHES are written above the staff. Strum chords in the rhythm indicated. Use the chord diagrams found at the top of the first page of the transcription for the appropriate chord voicings. Round noteheads indicate single notes.

THE MUSICAL STAFF shows pitches and rhythms and is divided by bar lines into measures. Pitches are named after the first seven letters of the alphabet.

TABLATURE graphically represents the guitar fingerboard. Each horizontal line represents a a string, and each number represents a fret.

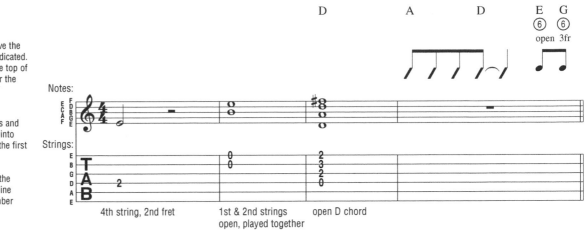

4th string, 2nd fret

1st & 2nd strings open, played together

open D chord

Definitions for Special Guitar Notation

HALF-STEP BEND: Strike the note and bend up 1/2 step.

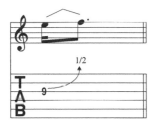

WHOLE-STEP BEND: Strike the note and bend up one step.

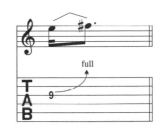

GRACE NOTE BEND: Strike the note and bend up as indicated. The first note does not take up any time.

SLIGHT (MICROTONE) BEND: Strike the note and bend up 1/4 step.

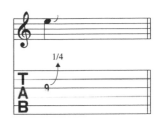

BEND AND RELEASE: Strike the note and bend up as indicated, then release back to the original note. Only the first note is struck.

PRE-BEND: Bend the note as indicated, then strike it.

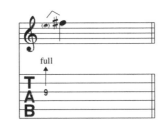

PRE-BEND AND RELEASE: Bend the note as indicated. Strike it and release the bend back to the original note.

UNISON BEND: Strike the two notes simultaneously and bend the lower note up to the pitch of the higher.

VIBRATO: The string is vibrated by rapidly bending and releasing the note with the fretting hand.

WIDE VIBRATO: The pitch is varied to a greater degree by vibrating with the fretting hand.

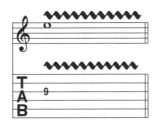

HAMMER-ON: Strike the first (lower) note with one finger, then sound the higher note (on the same string) with another finger by fretting it without picking.

PULL-OFF: Place both fingers on the notes to be sounded. Strike the first note and without picking, pull the finger off to sound the second (lower) note.

LEGATO SLIDE: Strike the first note and then slide the same fret-hand finger up or down to the second note. The second note is not struck.

SHIFT SLIDE: Same as legato slide, except the second note is struck.

TRILL: Very rapidly alternate between the notes indicated by continuously hammering on and pulling off.

TAPPING: Hammer ("tap") the fret indicated with the pick-hand index or middle finger and pull off to the note fretted by the fret hand.

NATURAL HARMONIC: Strike the note while the fret-hand lightly touches the string directly over the fret indicated.

PINCH HARMONIC: The note is fretted normally and a harmonic is produced by adding the edge of the thumb or the tip of the index finger of the pick hand to the normal pick attack.

HARP HARMONIC: The note is fretted normally and a harmonic is produced by gently resting the pick hand's index finger directly above the indicated fret (in parentheses) while the pick hand's thumb or pick assists by plucking the appropriate string.

PICK SCRAPE: The edge of the pick is rubbed down (or up) the string, producing a scratchy sound.

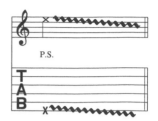

MUFFLED STRINGS: A percussive sound is produced by laying the fret hand across the string(s) without depressing, and striking them with the pick hand.

PALM MUTING: The note is partially muted by the pick hand lightly touching the string(s) just before the bridge.

RAKE: Drag the pick across the strings indicated with a single motion.

TREMOLO PICKING: The note is picked as rapidly and continuously as possible.

ARPEGGIATE: Play the notes of the chord indicated by quickly rolling them from bottom to top.

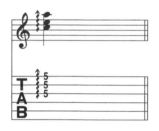

VIBRATO BAR DIVE AND RETURN: The pitch of the note or chord is dropped a specified number of steps (in rhythm) then returned to the original pitch.

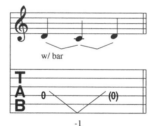

VIBRATO BAR SCOOP: Depress the bar just before striking the note, then quickly release the bar.

VIBRATO BAR DIP: Strike the note and then immediately drop a specified number of steps, then release back to the original pitch.

Additional Musical Definitions

(accent)	• Accentuate note (play it louder)	
(accent)	• Accentuate note with great intensity	
(staccato)	• Play the note short	
	• Downstroke	
V	• Upstroke	
D.S. al Coda	• Go back to the sign (%), then play until the measure marked "*To Coda*," then skip to the section labelled "*Coda*."	
D.S. al Fine	• Go back to the beginning of the song and play until the measure marked "*Fine*" (end).	

Rhy. Fig. • Label used to recall a recurring accompaniment pattern (usually chordal).

Riff • Label used to recall composed, melodic lines (usually single notes) which recur.

Fill • Label used to identify a brief melodic figure which is to be inserted into the arrangement.

Rhy. Fill • A chordal version of a Fill.

tacet • Instrument is silent (drops out).

• Repeat measures between signs.

• When a repeated section has different endings, play the first ending only the first time and the second ending only the second time.

NOTE: Tablature numbers in parentheses mean:
1. The note is being sustained over a system (note in standard notation is tied), or
2. The note is sustained, but a new articulation (such as a hammer-on, pull-off, slide or vibrato begins, or
3. The note is a barely audible "ghost" note (note in standard notation is also in parentheses).